the joy of machine embroidery

Face quilt hanging, *Elizabeth S. Gurrier.*
Photo, Robert Raiche.

the joy of machine embroidery

by regina bartley

HENRY REGNERY COMPANY · CHICAGO

Witch, *Margaret Cusack.*

Library of Congress Cataloging in Publication Data

Bartley, Regina.
  The joy of machine embroidery.

  Includes index.
  1.   Embroidery, Machine.   I.   Title.
TT772.B37   746.4'4   76-6259
ISBN 0-8092-8346-8

To Christopher Cross,
without whom this book
would not have been possible,
and
to my son, Ivan.

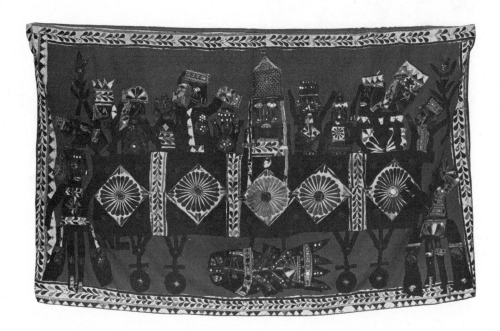

Persian Banquet, *Norman Laliberte,*
Courtesy Arras Gallery, New York.

Copyright © 1976 by Regina Bartley
All rights reserved
Published by Henry Regnery Company
180 North Michigan Avenue, Chicago, Illinois 60601
Manufactured in the United States of America
Library of Congress Catalog Card Number: 76-6259
International Standard Book Number: 0-8092-8346-8 (cloth)
                                     0-8092-7966-5 (paper)

Published simultaneously in Canada by
Beaverbooks
953 Dillingham Road
Pickering, Ontario L1W 1Z7
Canada

contents

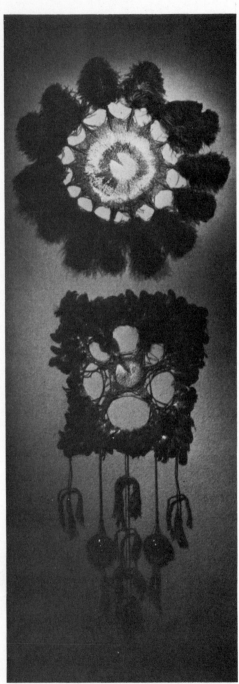

Feathered Totem, *Everett K. Sturgeon.*
Photo, Grover Gilchrist.

acknowledgments

Acknowledgments for *The Joy of Machine Embroidery* must start with my Bernina sewing machine. Almost with human understanding of the task ahead, my Bernina has responded as a friend to my every demand for endless varieties of stitch possibilities.

Then there are the creative artists who, in their search for new possibilities for self-expression, have made machine embroidery into a creative art form. Their experiments and creative output have been an inspiration to me. I hope their use of machine embroidery as an art form will serve as inspiration too for the millions of all ages who want to take their sewing to new heights using color, design, and form through machine embroidery.

To the American Home Sewing Council, the national nonprofit organization for the home sewing industry; to the Simplicity Pattern Company; to The Swiss Bernina Sewing Machine Company; and to the American Crafts Council, my gratitude for their encouragement and assistance.

Thanks to Melvyn T. Reiter for his many photographs of embroidered items.

A very special thanks to my son, Ivan, for his cooperation and understanding. And, finally, thanks go to Charlotte Porson, Loris Blake, Stephanie Natta, and others whose expressions of interest provided invaluable encouragement.

introduction

This is your recipe book—not for the kitchen, but for your sewing room or corner. Here you will find everything you need to know to enter the exciting, colorful, practical, and rewarding world of machine embroidery.

These easy-to-follow instructions and diagrams are all the ingredients; they'll give you all the skill and knowledge you need to become an artist at the sewing machine. There are simple but comprehensive charts to show you what needles and threads to use, and when. Detailed fabric charts explain precisely and clearly the many uses of various fabrics, with particular attention to machine embroidery. And endless stitch possibilities are clearly explained and diagramed, waiting for you to discover them.

EMBROIDERY IN FASHION AND DECORATING HISTORY

There was a time when only royalty and the very rich could afford to use embroidered objects every day. The hand embroidery commissioned by kings and noblemen, painstakingly produced by artists, has become the precious possession of famous museums around the world. One of the oldest arts, embroidery works are preserved in such institutions as the fascinating Victoria and Albert Museum in London. Embroidery is believed to predate even weaving; early peoples embroidered clothes made of skins.

Beautiful needlework has been associated with the Orient for centuries. Many years before Christ, Hebrew women, known as talented embroiderers, elaborately decorated their otherwise simple clothes and the fabrics for their homes. Etruscan women, who made costume history with their unique dress of tiny boleros over bare bosoms and long skirts, made their clothes more provocative still with embroideries.

Mushroom & Flowers *shorts, Linda Sampson.*
Photo, Vince Aiosa.

When silk came to Byzantium from China in the sixth century, this precious fiber was immediately adopted by royalty. But silk was not enough: it had to be made richer still with elaborate embroideries of gold and precious jewels. Even the royal feet were shod with silken slippers embroidered in dainty motifs. And, not to be outdone, the powerful and prestigious Church ordered lavish stitchery for ecclesiastical robes.

All this was before the advent of the sewing machine. Craftsmen devoted their whole lives to the production of fabulous works for royalty and church. One room was decorated for a queen with more than 1,000 gold-embroidered parakeets and more than 500 butterflies, their wings etched in gold embroidery. Birds and butterflies have remained among the most popular embroidery motifs to this day.

Another contemporary theme also had its beginning a thousand years ago, in dresses that were embroidered with phrases or songs—some holy, some naughty. These motifs were worked in gold and jewels on silk. Now, with the help of the sewing machine, the latest messages are stitched on T-shirts.

Several centuries later, when the fashion center shifted to Paris, embroiderers contributed to the luxury of royal life at 18th-century Versailles. Lavish dress was banished with the French Revolution in favor of natural dress. But fashion dies hard, and simple clothes began to cry for a bit of trim. Embroidery was one of the answers.

Fashion plates of the early nineteenth century show embroidered velvet shawls over mousseline dresses, embroidered silk stoles over afternoon dresses, evening dresses with all-over embroidery. With the Industrial Revolution came commercial machine embroidery, invented in Switzerland in 1846. It was an invention that brought the art within reach for everyone.

Throughout the centuries, while the ruling classes wore only the richest of embroideries, the common people developed their own styles. Instead of gold threads and jewels, they crafted their designs in colorful cotton threads, using all manner of adornments for their clothes. Even today peasant embroidery, especially for festival and special occasion costumes, is treasured in many countries.

WHAT THIS BOOK CAN MEAN TO YOU

Now, with this book and your own sewing machine, you can become an embroidery artist. Whether you have an old machine without attachments or a modern wonder with push-button magic, you'll discover that it is really a most important home appliance—an invaluable machine that can, with your skill and creativity, produce color, beauty, and excitement for you and your family.

You'll discover how you can transform any pattern into a boutique original. You'll see how easy it is to give any room a smart decorator look. You'll learn how easy it is to transform simple objects—draperies, pillows, place mats, and other household items

—into stunning works of art. Your home will reflect your personality in a way you never dreamed possible.

And there's even more to it than that—not only does machine embroidery give you self-satisfaction and the thrill of accomplishment, it also saves money. With this book and your sewing machine you can easily recreate clothes you've abandoned to the attic into exciting new clothes your whole family will love. And toys and gifts don't have to be expensive when you use your machine for embroidery.

The possibilities are endless. You could develop a marketable item, and make money as well as saving it. You could develop an art form and see your work exhibited in galleries: at the Crafts Museum in New York City entire exhibitions have been devoted to "Sewn Art," "The Embroidered Object," "Sewing as an Art Form."

With *The Joy of Machine Embroidery* as your guide and reference, your skill and your confidence will grow together. This practical, step-by-step guide gives you hundreds of machine embroidery projects to choose from, all planned and tested to assure your success. Make it your sewing companion, and use it frequently—for it is through use and familiarity that you will truly learn the joy of machine embroidery.

five easy projects

These five projects are a good way to launch into your embroidery discoveries and to broaden your awareness of the many applications of machine embroidery. They're fast and easy to do with simple straight stitches, and you can take off from the basic projects and create your own designs. Here are a few basic hints for embroidery success:

1. When you're first beginning, keep your designs simple.

2. When stitching a curved line, operate your machine slowly and turn your fabric gently.

3. When an angle is necessary, keep your needle down in the fabric as you turn it. Be sure to lower the presser foot before you start stitching again.

4. Your machine and bobbin threads should be pulled back through the toes of your presser foot before you begin.

5. After you've made a few stitches on your design, cut off the excess threads behind the presser foot; otherwise you may catch the loose threads in your stitches.

6. Don't worry too much about slight irregularities of line—that's the beauty of hand work! Remember, the machine is your embroidery tool, as the brush is the painter's tool.

7. To measure for a border, if you wish it to be centered or equally divided,
    a. fold border end of fabric;
    b. mark fold with a pencilled dot;
    c. use a ruler to divide your space to be sure your design will fit;
    d. make pencilled dots and draw the lines of your embroidery pattern from dot to dot.

THE STRAIGHT STITCH AS EMBROIDERY
1. A SCARF FOR YOU

Your scarf can be a long rectangle or a square; the size is determined by your personal preference.

   Suggested soft cottons; after you have a little experience,
    fabrics: silk; black, white, or a solid color.

Technique: Hem the scarf with your machine, turning the hem twice for a neat appearance. Or, if you wish, fringe the ends for a gay, carefree look.

2. A HANDKERCHIEF FOR HIM

You'll be less inhibited if you practice on inexpensive cotton handkerchiefs first. If there is a design already woven into the handkerchief, use it to your advantage. For more individual handkerchiefs, you may want to cut squares from remnants and hem them.

3. SWIRLING, DANGLING FUN DECORATIONS FOR THE CHILDREN OR THE FAMILY ROOM

For this project, a mobile, gaily patterned fabric is as desirable as solid colors. You may want to mix a variety of fabrics. This is a good time to hunt in your fabric scrap box or among your remnants for interesting choices.

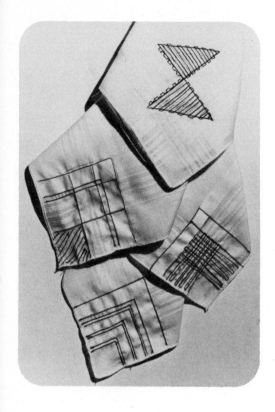

Technique: 1. The whole secret of making a mobile shape is to place a stiff piece of buckram between two layers of fabric that have been stitched on three sides and turned inside out. Place right sides together when stitching; the buckram should be about the size of the fabric after stitching. Tuck in the fabric edges and stitch the fourth side after you insert the buckram.

2. If your machine will sew through several layers of fabric, stitch your designs on last. If not, stitch them on before assembling the pieces.

3. Make several shapes—squares, rectangles, or triangles—and hang them on different-length strings; colored strings are pretty. Attach the strings to a stick or to two sticks tied in the middle to form an X.

4. PLACE MATS

Embroidered squares quickly become place mats, table covers, or marvelous pillows.

Suggested fabrics: linen-look rayon polyester or cotton polyester; black, white, or solid colors. This fabric is extremely easy to work with and will show up your design well.

Suggested size: twenty-one by fourteen inches.

Technique: Sew a 1½-inch hem at each end for a rectangle eighteen by fourteen inches. Fringe the other two sides about half an inch in; you can allow one inch extra fabric for hemming if desired. Stitch the hem in the same color thread you intend to use for your pattern stitches, to integrate it into the total design. The wider hem at the ends gives your embroidery a more substantial look.

5. POT HOLDERS

Make your own delightful pot holder, or a pin cushion, in one quick, easy sitting.

Technique: This is made like the mobile. Just insert padding instead of buckram and attach a loop on one corner.

 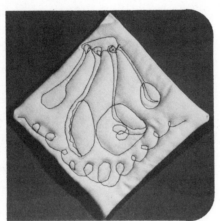

setting up a workshop

The first and most important thing to consider for your embroidery studio is comfort and convenience. This can be achieved with a bit of ingenuity, at little expense, in a corner of a room or in a specially adapted closet area. As machine embroidery requires few materials in addition to your sewing machine, a thrifty, well-set-up small area can prove as satisfactory and pleasant as an elaborate one with no expense spared. No matter what size your working area is, your storage space must be adequate and well planned.

HOW TO GET THE MOST OUT OF YOUR SPACE

Getting the most out of your space requires careful examination of your home. Ask yourself these questions:

Is there a corner of a room that can be set up as a permanent embroidery workshop?

Is there a closet that can be permanently organized for embroidering convenience?

Is there an area where you can keep a mobile embroidery workshop when it's not in use?

THE CORNER WORKSHOP

If the answer to the first question is yes, here are some suggestions to help you use your room space wisely. Wall shelves are a great floor space saver, and make a convenient storage place for your fabrics. Displayed in this way, they are both attractive to see and appealing to reach for and embroider.

There are other advantages to wall shelves. Storing fabrics in a closet or a drawer or under a bed increases the odds that you'll forget about them; locate your materials accessibly and you will be stimulated by their beauty. Having a place to put your fabrics also encourages you to take advantage of sales and to buy any interesting remnants you may chance to see—and most good buys are there only once. Take advantage of them—having fabrics at hand can be a money-saver as well as an inspiration to create your own embroidery.

How to Make Your Shelves

1. Install simple vertical strips with metal brackets.

2. On the brackets lay one-by-ten boards, precut from a lumber company. The length is determined by available space. Use brackets every three feet.

3. If desired, stain or paint the shelves to blend with your room decor.

4. You may prefer to attach separate brackets directly to the wall for shelf support. However, this is more work, and shelves made this way are not adjustable.

5. Ready-made storage cabinets can also be hung attractively.

How you arrange your shelves, of course, depends upon available space and the time and money you want to spend. The accompanying illustrations show what can be done with an easy-to-construct workshop and with a more elaborate setup.

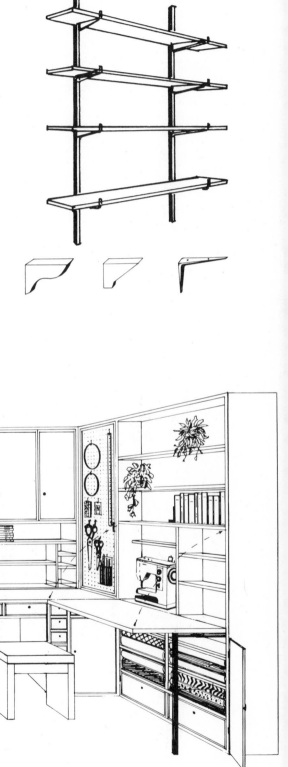

Illustrations by Charlotte Porson

THE CLOSET WORKSHOP

1. Shelves can be hung on the back of a closet door, close to your sewing area.

2. Put a front strip across these shelves, as the door movement may disturb the fabric. The shelves are shallow, so tack a small strip of wood across the front to create a bin-like effect.

3. Hanging a shallow cabinet on the inside of a closet door is another excellent way to have additional storage space for fabrics.

4. Bars like towel racks can be another easy space-saving way to store fabrics on the back of a closet door. You'll have room for several bars.

5. If your closet is large enough, and not needed for other purposes, the whole closet can be turned into a work storage space. Hinge an ironing board to the door.

6. A small conventional closet can be converted so that all usable space is easily accessible. Just remove the door and enlarge the door opening as much as possible. Then add a larger door frame to permit you to hang double doors. These double doors will give your closet area a much more spacious feeling. You may wish to eliminate the doors altogether for an alcove effect.

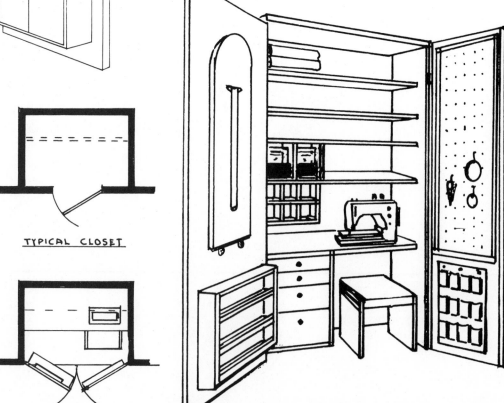

TYPICAL CLOSET

The Closet Door Unit

Finally, if your closet is not adaptable inside for an embroidery workshop or if you prefer working in the larger space of the room, you can use the outside of the closet door to create shelves or a complete combination work-storage space.

1. Attach shelves to the outside of the closet door.

2. At table height, nail a strip of wood across the shelves.

3. Hinge to the strip a plywood panel that will cover the shelves when lifted. Put a hook on each side to hold the panel in place.

4. Hinge a second smaller panel one-third of the way down from the top of the first panel. When lowered the second panel serves as a support for the first panel and creates a sewing table. This panel can also have a shallow cabinet for threads and other miscellany.

5. The lower area can be covered with a single door or double doors made of simple plywood and hinged on. To complete the cabinet, add a pretty knob.

6. The area below the table panel can serve as additional storage space; it makes a perfect place to keep a portable sewing machine.

7. The entire cabinet structure can be painted. This type of structure can also be attached to a wall or a bookcase.

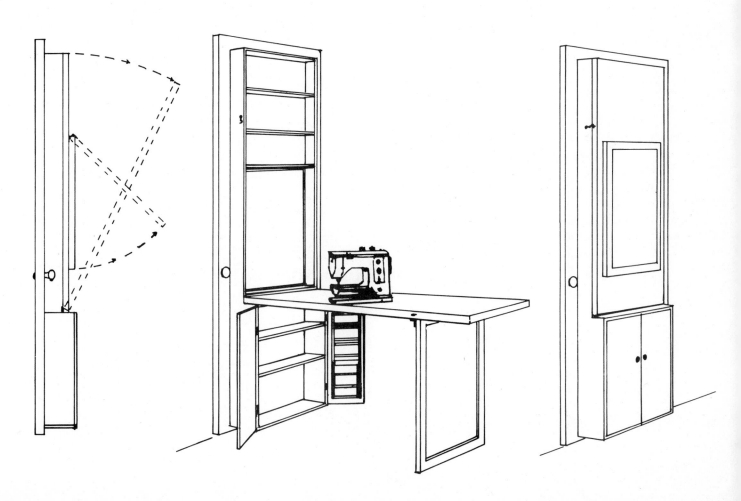

THE MOBILE WORKSHOP

Among the many desirable features of a mobile embroidery workshop is the obvious one: you can move it, not only within one room but from room to room. You can store it in a large closet—plan the dimensions in advance so it will fit easily. You can make it attractive enough for the living room, the family room, or a bedroom. And it can be designed to serve several functions.

1. The basic structure is a shallow vertical or horizontal box.

2. Construct the box with a section that drops or lifts to form a table.

3. Build storage shelves or drawers inside.

The dimensions will depend on your needs; here are a few possibilities.

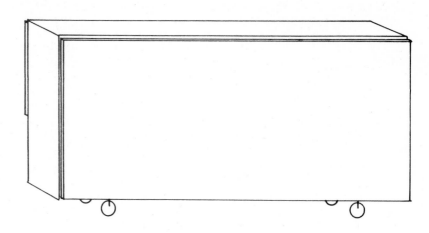

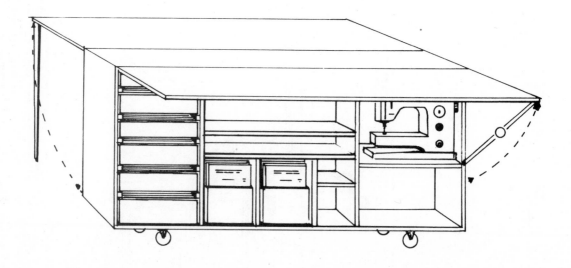

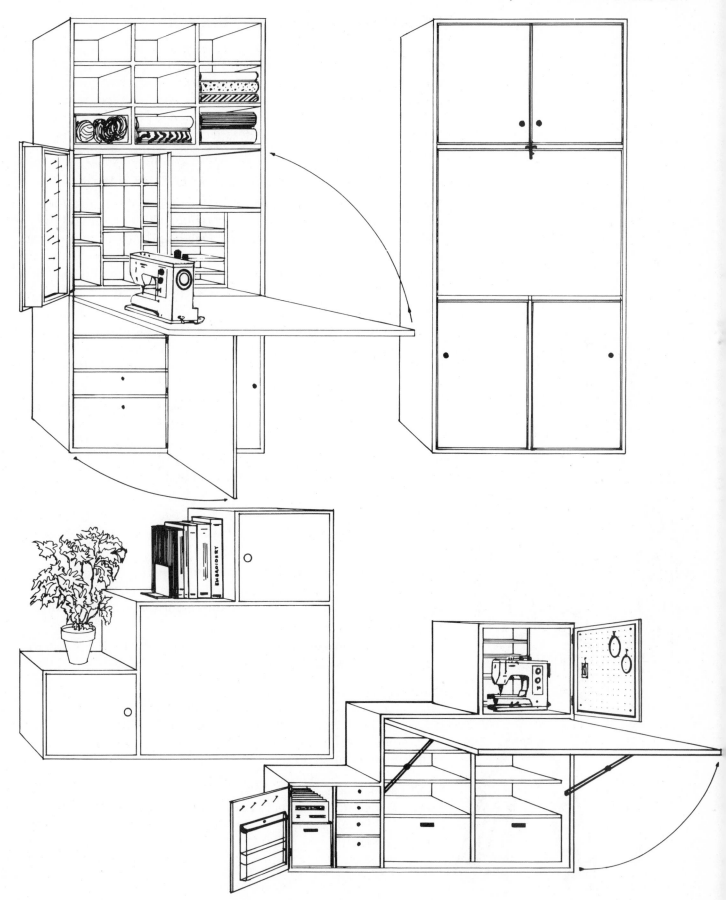

ORGANIZING YOUR WORKSHOP

If you have a machine or a sewing table with drawers, organize according to categories—for example, needles and threads and small items in the top drawer, scissors and embroidery hoops in another, machine books, patterns, and machine attachments in the largest. If you have a portable machine or need more space than the drawers afford, here are some detailed suggestions to help you organize.

KEEPING YOUR EMBROIDERY TOOLS CLOSE AT HAND

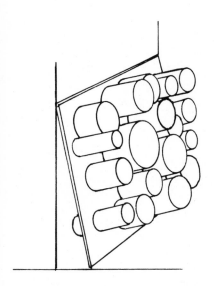

A wonderfully convenient and attractive means of keeping your constantly used tools handy is a board hung like a picture on the wall near your machine. A well-arranged board can be an ornament as well as a time-saver. Make your tool board of wood with nails to hang things on; of pegboard with hooks to hang things on; of cloth with pockets to put things in; or of cans glued to a board and tilted slightly.

When you've decided on the arrangement of your tool board, hang each item in its place and outline it with a marker. This will help you return each tool to its proper spot when you've finished using it.

Thread

As you'll want many colors of thread for machine embroidery, your spools should be easy to see and easy to reach. Ready-made spool racks or holders are not too expensive. Some of these fit into a sewing machine drawer; some are tiered, and can almost triple your shelf space. However, if you want to spend little or no money, make your own spool tree.

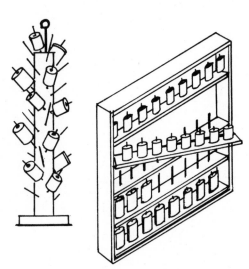

1. Use a one-by-one or one-by-two piece of wood, its length depending on your space and taste. One and a half feet is a good average. Attach it to a square base.

2. Drive two-inch finishing nails into the stick at three- or four-inch intervals. The nails should slant up. If you use a one-by-two, drive two rows of nails slanting outwards as well as upwards.

3. A screw eye at the top of your spool tree will enable you to hang it on the wall near your machine or in a storage area.

Patterns

When handled with care, patterns can be used again and again, so it's wise to keep them together in a special box. This box can be decorative as well as useful, if it is painted or covered with wallpaper or contact paper.

Small Tool Holders

An embroidery tool apron is a good way to keep the little things handy; simply add pockets to any apron. A carpenter's canvas apron can also be useful.

A bulletin board near your embroidery area can be a good place to keep notes of embroidery ideas. You may also find it inspirational to have a file folder or box for newspaper or magazine clippings.

And for the small things you use most frequently, you can make an embroidery tool kit with pockets just the right size. When not needed, just roll it up and put it away until the next time.

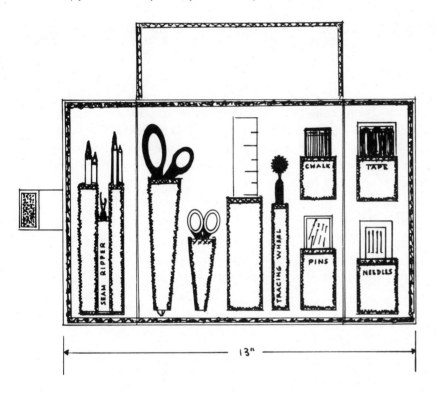
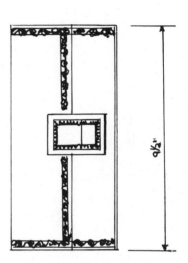

chapter 3

the sewing machine

Selecting a sewing machine that will best serve your needs should be done with care and informed awareness. You should know what to look for and why. Chosen wisely, your machine can prove to be a treasured tool for many years—one that will enrich your wardrobe, your home, and your life.

THE MACHINE

A most important part of your sewing machine, especially for machine embroidering, is the needle. How the needle moves determines largely what your machine can do.

There are two basic types of needle movement:

The *lockstitch machine* has a needle that moves up and down in a straight line only.

The *zigzag machine* has a swing needle that moves from side to side with controlled stitch width and length.

When the zigzag machine was first introduced in Europe, home sewing was revolutionized. The zigzag machine can do many things previously done by hand. It sews on buttons, makes professional-looking buttonholes—and, of course, embroiders. Embroidery was no longer a painstaking, time-consuming affair but an almost magically fast machine process.

I have found the Bernina sewing machine from Switzerland to be the most trouble-free; this is the one I have used throughout this book. Its twenty decorative stitch patterns are built right into the machine, and are, therefore, fully automatic. It is only necessary to flip a switch and embroider. It can sew on buttons and make perfect buttonholes of any length; it can blind-stitch, hemstitch, shell-edge, and cord-edge. It can tailor-tack and fagot. These are just a few of its possibilities; they require only that the presser foot be changed.

Two distinctly different types of lower arms are available on sewing machines today:

The *flatbed arm* is a low bed level with the sewing table.

The *free lower arm* has space all around it and is marvelous for hard-to-get-at places.

The free lower arm, like the zigzag machine, was first developed in Europe. I find it especially helpful for embroidering pants legs, decorating sleeves, or enhancing simple socks. My Bernina also has a table extension that attaches easily around the free arm. This gives me a wide sewing surface that is both convenient and comfortable.

CHOOSING A SEWING MACHINE

When you choose your next sewing machine, be sure that it has *at least* these features:

- A lever for sewing forward and reverse.
- A clear tension adjuster.
- A hinged presser foot—this facilitates sewing over seams and pins.
- A feed dog that is easy to drop or has a special plate for free embroidery. Covering the feed dog is less desirable than dropping it, as it may leave a bump. This can prevent the easy flow of fabric necessary for fine work.
- A bobbin winder that is self-releasing and easy to use. I find that the Bernina bobbin spool not only winds easily, it holds so much thread it is not necessary to stop in the middle of my embroidering and rewind.
- A bobbin that is easy to place in the machine—my machine has a snagproof bobbin case that is jam-free so loose threads can't get inside and cause trouble.
- Easy threading. This is especially desirable, when embroidering, for changing the thread color.
- A well-placed, efficient thread cutter, to save time and scissor hunting.

These are the minimum necessary. You will also find it advantageous for machine embroidery if the machine you choose has these features:

- The motor should be adjustable. It can be a distinct asset to be able to reduce the speed of your machine for embroidering; this is essential for eyelets and cut work.
- The machine should be capable of sewing over several layers of fabrics. As my machine is especially adapted to this, I find it invaluable for appliqué and quilting.
- The machine should be portable if space is limited.

And in a zigzag machine, the most desirable for machine embroidery, also look for these features:

- A well-designed, convenient stitch width control.
- A well-designed, convenient stitch length control. I find that I can achieve a much wider range of design possibilities simply by turning my Bernina's stitch length knob while embroidering with its built-in patterns.
- An easy-to-move, well-placed needle position lever.

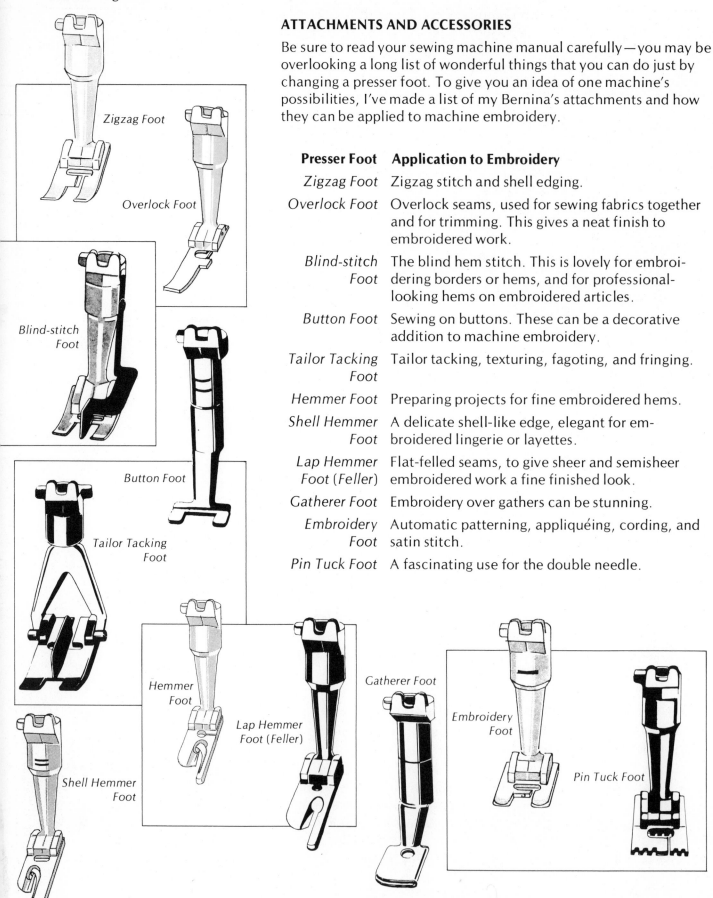

ATTACHMENTS AND ACCESSORIES

Be sure to read your sewing machine manual carefully—you may be overlooking a long list of wonderful things that you can do just by changing a presser foot. To give you an idea of one machine's possibilities, I've made a list of my Bernina's attachments and how they can be applied to machine embroidery.

Presser Foot	Application to Embroidery
Zigzag Foot	Zigzag stitch and shell edging.
Overlock Foot	Overlock seams, used for sewing fabrics together and for trimming. This gives a neat finish to embroidered work.
Blind-stitch Foot	The blind hem stitch. This is lovely for embroidering borders or hems, and for professional-looking hems on embroidered articles.
Button Foot	Sewing on buttons. These can be a decorative addition to machine embroidery.
Tailor Tacking Foot	Tailor tacking, texturing, fagoting, and fringing.
Hemmer Foot	Preparing projects for fine embroidered hems.
Shell Hemmer Foot	A delicate shell-like edge, elegant for embroidered lingerie or layettes.
Lap Hemmer Foot (Feller)	Flat-felled seams, to give sheer and semisheer embroidered work a fine finished look.
Gatherer Foot	Embroidery over gathers can be stunning.
Embroidery Foot	Automatic patterning, appliquéing, cording, and satin stitch.
Pin Tuck Foot	A fascinating use for the double needle.

Zigzag Foot

Overlock Foot

Blind-stitch Foot

Button Foot

Tailor Tacking Foot

Hemmer Foot

Lap Hemmer Foot (Feller)

Shell Hemmer Foot

Gatherer Foot

Embroidery Foot

Pin Tuck Foot

Single Hem-stitch Needle	With the embroidery foot on fine fabrics; ruche, appliqué with pre-embroidered materials, and trellis work with metallic thread. This is also useful for borders, good for decorating linens and women's fashions. NOTE: For an attractive effect, try leading a double metallic thread up through the hole in the embroidery foot.
Double Hemstitch Needle	With the embroidery foot; everything from zigzag to fancy hemstitching.
Eyelet Embroidery Foot *Special Needle Plate* *Slides, two sizes* *Round awl* *Square awl*	All accessories combined; eyelet or English embroidery.
Knee Lever	This special accessory raises the presser foot without the use of the hands, a valuable feature for machine embroidery.

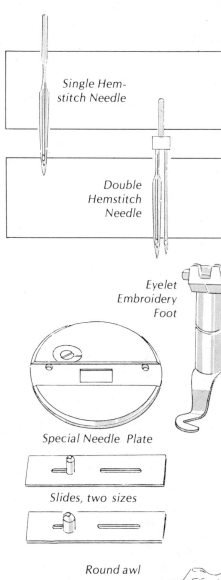

Single Hem-stitch Needle

Double Hemstitch Needle

Eyelet Embroidery Foot

Special Needle Plate

Slides, two sizes

Round awl

Square awl

Knee Lever

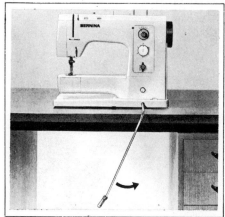

THREADS AND NEEDLES

THREADS

Machine embroidery thread, which is made of mercerized cotton, is more flexible and finer than the same number in regular sewing thread. It comes in three sizes: number 30, number 50, and number 60. No. 30 m.e. is similar to a regular No. 50 sewing thread—but the No. 30 m.e. is more pliable.

Machine embroidery thread has a lovely sheen. Since it is mercerized cotton, it stretches less than silk thread, and much less than wool thread. While synthetic threads are recommended for working on synthetic *fabrics,* they are not good for embroidery. Cotton is still the best, as polyester makes up very stiff and hard.

NOTE: Use a thick wool thread on a shiny satin surface or a metallic thread on a wool fabric to achieve lovely contrasts. Wind the heavier thread in the bobbin spool or use the couching technique, joining the threads to the fabric surface with a zigzag or a pattern stitch.

The bobbin spool, as indicated above, offers a very wide range of embroidery possibilities. Threads used in the bobbin can be thicker and heavier than those in the needle. If it is impossible to machine-wind them, they can be hand-wound. Even hand embroidery threads and novelty wools can be used in this manner. Always be careful to wind the thread on the bobbin firmly and evenly, without twisting.

In general, always remember:

• Bobbin thread should be thinner than the needle thread, if possible, to reduce bulk. Use No. 30 on top, for example, and No. 60 in the bobbin.

• For regular and free embroidery, if you wish the bobbin thread to show more on the finished embroidery than the needle thread, work from the wrong side of the fabric.

NEEDLES

For machine embroidery you will most use the number 11 needle (70 in Europe) or the number 14 needle (80 in Europe). To avoid fraying and breaking of the thread, be sure that the needle and the thread correspond. Check the table below.

Fabric Weight	Very Fine to Fine	Medium to Heavy	Heaviest
Needle	11 (70)	14 (80)	16 (90)
Mercerized Sewing Thread (3-ply)	50	50	40
Machine Embroidery Thread (2-ply)	60-50 (60)	50	30

NOTE: For wools, knits, and synthetics use an equivalent ballpoint needle.

WORKING WITH YOUR MACHINE

For best machine performance and embroidery pleasure, keep your machine in good working order:

• Be sure you have read your machine manual carefully so that you understand the machine's parts, accessories, and attachments.

• Always keep your machine manual handy so you can check it when you're uncertain.

• Keep your machine clean and brush it free of dust and fluff often. Cover when not in use.

• Keep your machine well oiled; otherwise it will run hard and noisily.

• Lower the presser foot lever when sewing and embroidering, even if the foot is removed. This maintains the thread tension.

• Use the proper presser foot for best results.

• Wind the bobbin correctly—not too full.

• Check for correct threading of machine and needle.

• The needle must be sharp and straight.

• The needle must match the thread. If the needle is too fine, the thread will fray and break.

• Be sure to place the needle in the machine correctly. Check your manual if you are unsure of how to do this.

• For threading ease, cut the thread at an angle and put a piece of white paper behind the needle eye. The white behind the needle makes it easier to see the eye.

• On some machines, trying to sew through heavy fabric or several layers of fabric will break the thread.

• If you're using an embroidery hoop, be sure the fabric is stretched tightly.

• Sewing too many stitches or sewing too quickly in free embroidery without moving the fabric will result in thread breakage.

• If you pull the fabric against the needle, the needle will break.

• Try not to move the hoop too quickly, as it will snap the thread.

• If the fabric is not held flat to the sewing machine bed when the presser foot is removed, the needle will not pick up the bobbin thread.

Increased familiarity with your machine and its capabilities will make you relaxed and confident. Your sewing machine will become a friend, one you get to know and work with in harmony and productivity.

chapter 4

a wealth of stitches

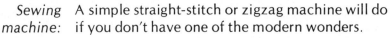

Embroidery stitches are the language, the vocabulary of machine embroidery, and there is a great variety of stitches to choose from. In this chapter, stitches are explained and illustrated. These special practice exercises will help you gain confidence, will make you familiar with simple stitches and the many combinations you can create. The most important thing, as you may have learned from the suggested straight-stitch projects, is to experiment.

Here are the materials you need:

Sewing machine: A simple straight-stitch or zigzag machine will do if you don't have one of the modern wonders.

Fabric: Use ten-by-ten-inch squares of various fabric. Remnants and scraps can be useful and money-saving. Muslin is excellent; burlap, gauze, cotton, linen, silk, wool, and synthetics (like Arnel, polyester, knits) are suggested to widen your stitch possibilities. Different fabrics react differently to embroidering, so be sure to use a variety of weights and textures.

Scissors: Use the sharp-pointed embroidery type for cutting threads, and regular cutting shears for cutting fabric.

Thread: D.M.C., Swiss-Metrosene, Mettler, Coats & Clark, and Anchor machine embroidery thread, No. 30 or No. 50 mercerized cotton, are recommended. These threads are available in a variety of colors. Try experimenting with different threads, too—polyester, silk and any others you may discover.

Embroidery hoop: Try a seven-inch hoop first; you may eventually want several sizes.

Stiffening: Spray starch, typing paper, and iron-on products are all useful. Use starch on washables only, typing paper under any fabric. Pellon, Stitch-Witchery, Vilene, and others, ironed onto the back of the fabric, are expecially suitable for knits and doubleknits. They can be left on or steamed off.

Embroidery foot: This enables you to see your work more clearly as you embroider.

Try hoop and stiffeners singly or in combination to see what pleases you. Although you can embroider on fabric as is, you will be more pleased with the results when you use the suggested backings and the hoop. Heavier fabrics, like denim or twill, do not need backings.

BASIC EMBROIDERY TECHNIQUES

EXERCISE 1: Straight Stitching with Reverse

First try sewing in two directions: forward, reverse—forward, reverse. A lovely pattern will start to develop. Move the fabric to the left or right when reversing; you will find that you can control the pattern. Much variety can be achieved by changing the length of forward or reverse stitching or the amount of the turn, whether the turn is to the left or right. Go slowly; count; develop a rhythm.

EXERCISE 2: Geometric Designs in Straight Stitch

Pencil in a few parallel lines on the fabric and stitch along them. At the end of each line, keep the needle in the fabric, make a right-angle turn and stitch three stitches; keep the needle in the fabric and make another right-angle turn. Then stitch along the next line. Continue to do this and you will have a handsome geometric pattern. This same principle can be applied in a variety of design possibilities.

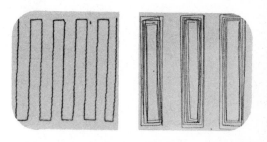

EXERCISE 3: Circular Stitching

Try turning your fabric in circles as the needle moves; a great variety of patterns can be traced.

EXERCISE 4: A Geometric Flower

Use a compass or trace around a few round shapes like small bottle tops or spools to make geometric flowers; straight stitch along the lines of the circles and at regular intervals make turns inward from the circle and back again, or reverse stitch towards the center and back again. A center can be stitched by slowly sewing around a small circle. Add a stem and a leaf by drawing them on with a soft pencil and straight-stitching over them, the leaves once and the stem twice.

EXERCISE 5: Free-Surface Machine Stitching

For a more exciting experiment, get out your embroidery hoop and

stretch a piece of fabric on it, about two or three inches longer than the hoop. Take off the presser foot of your machine. Be sure to lower the presser bar lever in order to have upper thread tension. Guide the hoop carefully by your fingertips. The feed dog should be down or covered with a plate if your machine requires it. On my Bernina it is only necessary to remove the presser foot. The feed dog can be lowered if desired. You can also thread the lower thread in the bobbin case or increase bobbin thread tension. Press gently on the controls of your machine. Sew two or three stitches and cut away excess thread. Turn the hooped fabric as you go and watch the patterns develop. The reverse side of the fabric can be equally interesting. The more you practice, the more control you'll gain and the more interesting your embroidery will be.

NOTE: To enrich your adventure with free-surface stitching, collect a few simple photos of natural subjects—flowers, birds, rocks, trees, and so on—and designs you like from magazines. Place on the wrong side of the fabric and outline with a simple straight stitch. This pattern can be turned over, placed on an embroidery hoop and elaborated on.

EXERCISE 6: Free-Surface Machine Embroidery with Varied Stitch Length and Width

You can achieve different effects by changing stitch length and width and machine tension; do not touch the bobbin tension. Slow movement of the fabric will result in short stitches, fast movement in long stitches. Shaped areas can be achieved by working in close rows. Often the reverse side of the fabric is more interesting than the right side. Try working with felt at first, as it requires no hoop or stiffener.

There are countless embroidery possibilities to try and to apply, and once you get started you'll gain confidence and do your own experimenting. When you've gained a repertoire of straight-stitch designs, explore the possibilities of the simple zigzag stitch. Be sure to use a stiffener or a hoop. Keep a record of your favorite designs, with notes pinned to them to log your procedures.

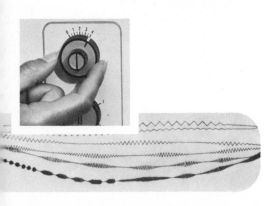

EXERCISE 7: Satin Stitch

By varying stitch width as you sew—I simply turn the Bernina's control left or right—a variety of designs can be achieved.

EXERCISE 8: Zigzag Free Stitch

Raise the presser foot and lightly hold fabric flat to machine or place in a hoop. As the needle moves, turn the fabric. It's pleasant to work to music and turn the fabric to its rhythms—a fascinating pattern can result.

EXERCISE 9: Zigzag with Maximum Stitch Width and Length

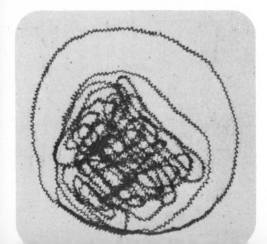

Do a row of zigzag stitches; turn the fabric, keeping the needle down. Make diamonds or stripes or irregular designs. Crossing over

the first rows of stitches in another direction gives interesting results; use contrasting colors of thread.

NOTE: Working like this without a stiffening agent in back gives the fabric a slight stretch or smocking quality.

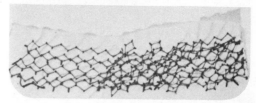

EXERCISE 10: Circular Zigzag with an Embroidery Hoop

Stitch, following the edge of the hoop and then the line formed by this action; continue stitching in a spiral until you reach the center. This is an excellent exercise for gaining control. Remember—a gentle pull by both hands to stretch the fabric will enhance the appearance of all of your embroidery designs.

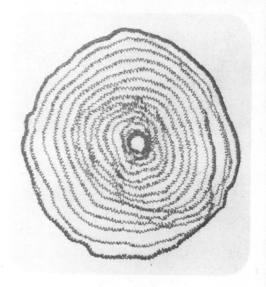

Finally, combine the confidence, skill, and knowledge gained from the exercises with the automatic patterning ability of your machine. The possibilities are endless. Many of these variations are recorded here for you to enjoy doing—to enjoy living with. The key is experimentation; only this can give you the confidence to design, to decorate, to create with your sewing machine.

A CATALOG OF STITCHES

THE STRAIGHT STITCH
See Exercises 1, 2, 3, 4, and 5.

The Basic Straight Stitch
Technique:
1. To avoid pucker, put typing paper under fabric.

2. Hold or pin together at intervals.

3. If a large piece of fabric, roll under and pin part not being embroidered for ease of handling; repin as necessary to keep fabric flat and pins out of working area.

4. As you straight stitch, turn and twist fabric; a design will result. Stitch slowly for more control.

5. If you wish, draw the design first. Practice first on a scrap of fabric.

Geometric Patterns and Free Lines
Technique:
1. Stitch forward and reverse, as explained in Exercise 1.

2. Make geometric designs with straight stitch, as explained in Exercise 2.

3. Free lines can be repeated to make a design; several thread colors can be used. At beginning and end of stitched line, a couple of forward and reverse stitches will secure thread.

Puckering with Tension Variations
Technique:
1. Tighten upper tension.

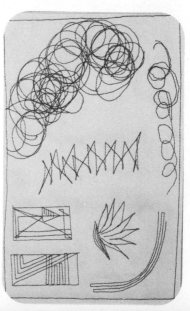

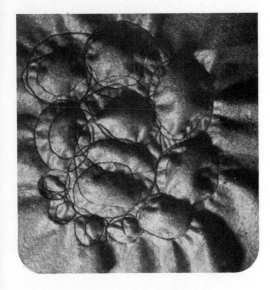

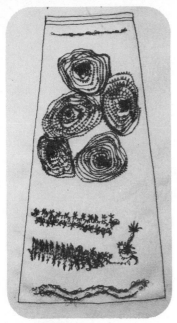

2. Proceed with free stitching. The tighter the tension, the higher the relief; experiment to find out what your machine can do.

3. Use a soft fabric like felt for best results.

4. Pattern stitching can be used in the low areas afterwards for a rich decorative effect.

THE ZIGZAG STITCH

See Exercises 6, 8, 9, and 10; also see Couching *and* Smocking and Gathering.

FREE-SURFACE MACHINE EMBROIDERY

See Exercise 5

Straight stitch with tension variation for textured effect, working from reverse side.

Technique: 1. Put fabric in embroidery hoop and stretch tight.

2. Loosen upper tension; lower tension can be tightened or lower thread threaded in bobbin case, but this is not necessary.

3. *Be sure to lower presser bar or lever when you remove presser foot!*

4. Feed dog can be up or down or covered.

5. Pull bobbin thread up through fabric. Use normal method of bringing up bobbin thread—turn hand wheel a little to release thread if necessary.

6. Start the machine—move hoop back and forth, left to right, *slowly* while stitching, or needle or thread will break.

7. Make three or four forward-reverse stitches to lock thread at beginning and end of stitching.

Straight stitch and zigzag with embroidery floss in bobbin. Upper and lower threads black. Be sure to lower tension lever.

Technique: TWO LOWER MOTIFS.

1. Draw your design or work freehand as you go. Move hoop gently and work machine slowly as you follow the line.

2. Do outline first; leave shapes free or fill in with lines.

Free-surface machine embroidery with straight stitch loops and lines, zigzag-textured filled-in dark center. Remember to work slowly for control and confidence.

Technique: CENTER.

1. To form loops, move the hoop from side to side backwards and forwards.

2. Press down very gently on hoop as you move it. Remember, jerky movements will break your thread or your needle.

3. Zigzag with yarn in bobbin. The dark center's heavy dark bar is worked from the end of the bar up; this order could be reversed. Hoop is moved gently from side to side towards machine, front and back again for a denser fill. The jagged points at the bottom are formed by moving the hoop back and forth and stitching at greater speed.

4. The open grille-like stitching in the center is also formed by rows of wider-spaced stitching.

5. The closer zigzag stitch at the top of this design is formed by moving only forward and backward, not side to side.

Zigzag with embroidery floss in bobbin case, not free-surface machine embroidery. Presser foot and feed dog are used.

Simple control is required for this type of regular zigzag. Notice the variety of design possibilities:

- spaced rows
- closer rows
- touching rows forming diamonds
- vertical rows on right
- vertical rows on left crossing horizontal rows

Zigzag with free-surface machine embroidery, floss in bobbin.

Technique: TOP.

Outside, series of freely worked zigzag stitch lines. Notice density variations. The movement of the hoop determines this—slower movement forward and backward, closer stitches, denser line, and vice versa.

OPEN LINES IN CENTER.

Formed in the same way, with side-to-side movements. The bobbin thread has been removed, giving the other side of the fabric an open looped texture. These loops can be protected from unraveling by pressing a no-iron product on side opposite loops.

The border is a simple straight stitch with embroidery floss in the bobbin. Interesting variations can be achieved by using contrasting colors for the spool and the bobbin thread.

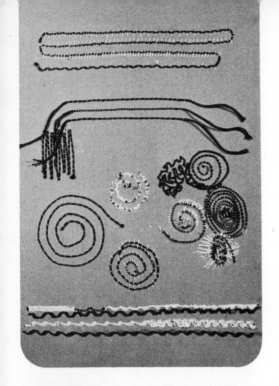

Lower the presser bar lever or thread will knot up; pull bobbin thread up to the side you're working on. Cut extra bobbin and spool threads after a few stitches; this avoids bunching it into your stitches. If necessary, stretch fabric into shape after stitching. Be sure to use hoop or back fabric; it's best to do both if possible. With knits, back only. Hold fabric firmly to machine, but move gently.

More texture with tension variations, embroidery floss wound on bobbin.

    Technique: LEFT SPIRAL.
       Not free-surface machine embroidery, tensions are equal.
       CENTER SPIRALS.
       Top, spool thread tension tighter; open pattern stitch used. Bottom, tension same as top spiral; zigzag stitch used.
       RIGHT SPIRALS.
       Top, not for free-surface machine embroidery; first black and then white bobbin thread used.
       CENTER.
       Left spiral, looser top tension than right spiral.
       BOTTOM.
       Looser bobbin tension.

Detail of motif from scarf, chapter 6.

Worked on net with embroidery floss in bobbin; use hoop. Work from reverse.

OPEN-SPACE STITCHING.

Use free-surface machine embroidery technique; later, practice with zigzag and pattern stitches. Line quality will differ.

    Technique: 1. Place fabric firmly in hoop.

       2. Work three rows of straight stitches in a circle just inside the hoop.

       3. Cut away fabric inside the circle (remove from machine to cut, if necessary). Fabric remains in hoop.

       4. Make a few securing stitches in the edge of the circle.

       5. Hold hoop to machine lightly; move it slowly while machine is stitching across the open side to the opposite edge. This may take practice; be sure presser bar lever is lowered.

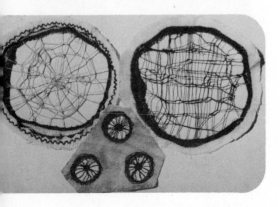

6. Stitch around the edge of the circle for half of the circumference.

7. Cross the open space again; you will have an X of free-stitched lines.

8. Repeat step 6 for one-fourth of the circumference of the circle, and then step 7. Repeat several times, stitching around one-eighth of the circumference and so on, to form the web.

9. New gently stitch across and around the web, forming patterns.

The web can be spoked or filled in with horizontal and vertical lines or anything else you invent. Your shapes can be asymmetrical as well as circular.

The outer edge can be free-surface machine embroidery, straight stitch, zigzag stitch, or a regular pattern stitch or satin stitch; a rich design can be stitched to border your open-space web. It can be integrated with the other designs or used as the main design on curtains, scarves and so on. Fine yarn or embroidery floss can be used in the bobbin to give you more substantial lines; the outer edge of the circle can be treated in the same way for a padded look. The sizes of the open shapes can vary, and the open spaces can also be backed with contrasting fabrics.

THE SATIN STITCH

Stitch length: almost 0
Stitch width: 1 to widest possible

Turning Corners

Straight corners.

Technique: 1. OPEN CORNER.
Leave space by leaving needle in fabric on inside edge; turn and continue to sew.

2. CLOSED CORNER.
Sew to corner. Leave needle at outer point; turn and continue to sew.

3. DIAGONAL DESIGN IN CORNER.
Sew as above, but when sewing in corner, slowly turn zigzag to 0. While sewing out, slowly turn zigzag to 4 again.

Curved corners.

Technique: 1. Design should be visible in lengthwise slot of embroidery foot.

2. Sew to corner.

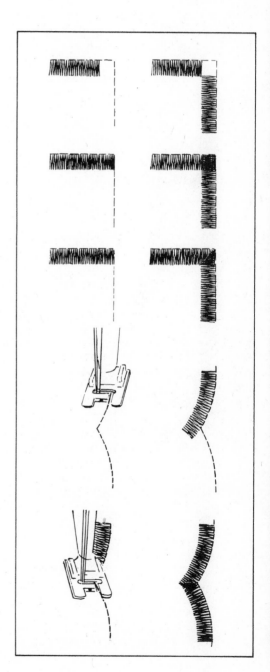

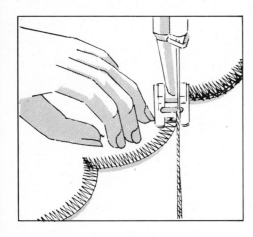

3. Raise foot; needle should be in fabric. Turn work, 2.2 or at 0. Lower foot; design should again be visible in slot.

4. Turn zigzag to 4 while sewing slowly.

Scalloped Borders

Technique: 1. Make a cardboard stencil and draw scallops.

2. Back with typing paper.

3. Sew satin stitch seam.

4. Remove paper; cut carefully around scallops.

5. Use zigzag to oversew edge.

6. Guide a pearl cord on edge; do not let it slide over or under.

7. Hold the border cord straight, and guide fabric slowly near the foot.

Straight Borders

Technique: 1. Back with paper; sew satin stitch seam. Remove paper and cut away excess fabric. Optional: oversew with zigzag, stitch width 2½ to 3, stitch length 1 to 1½, while guiding a pearl cord as for a scalloped border (A).

2. At the corner, lower feed dog and sew three stitches using the hand wheel. Raise foot, needle in work on inside edge. Turn work. Make a loop with the cord, lower foot, and sew three stitches; raise feed dog and continue sewing carefully. Pull cord end to make loop disappear (B). Push stitch over corner and continue sewing, with stitch width at 1½ and stitch length at ¼ .

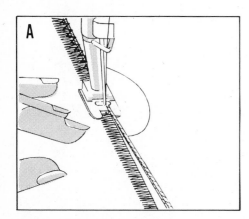

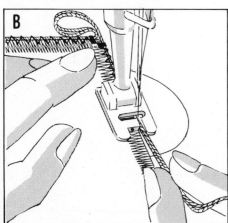

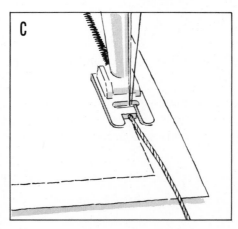

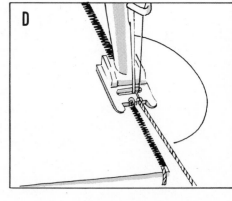

Narrow Borders

Technique: 1. Draw pearl yarn or embroidery floss through hole in embroidery foot, front to back. Sew seam with satin stitch (C). Cut away excess fabric carefully.

2. This step is optional, depending upon the desired effect. Set stitch width at 2 or 3 and stitch length at almost 0. With the small buttonhole foot, cover first satin stitch with a second; the satin stitch seam should be in the left slot of foot. Cord goes in right slot of foot. This enables you to join the yarn or floss exactly at the edge (D). Corners are made as above.

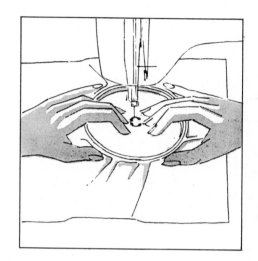

Other Possibilities

For line in design, look at the exercises and the straight stitch section for ideas—it's great for placemats and tablecloths.

For texture, satin stitch blocks can be stitched in different directions, to catch the light. Lines of satin stitch can be piled up for textured relief; they can cross each other, vertically and horizontally, and in different tones and colors. Lines of varying widths can be used close together for another kind of interest.

For fill-in of solid embroidered areas, see Free-surface Machine Embroidery section.

For monogramming, see chapter 12.

Technique: 1. Use the same preparation as for free-surface machine embroidery. Bring bobbin thread up through fabric, sew a few straight stitches, and cut thread ends. Set dials for stitch length 0, stitch width 2 to 4, as desired.

2. Make a test stitch; the pattern line must be in the middle of the zigzag.

3. Move the hoop as you sew, as if you were writing with it. Do not stop turning the hoop until the monogram is complete.

4. Hold the hoop as for darning, keeping fingers in one place and holding securely. Irregular movements produce uneven monograms; run machine quickly and guide hoop slowly and steadily.

For appliqué, use satin stitch to secure and accent shapes.

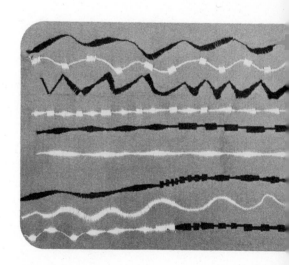

VARIED STITCH WIDTH SATIN STITCH

By turning the stitch width knob back and forth as you sew, with stitch length set at almost 0, you can develop many beautiful patterns. Counting as you go helps achieve repeat patterns; practice and develop a rhythm. Undulating lines and long thin leaves are easily achieved this way.

APPLIQUÉ

Suggested stitches:	Secure fabric shapes with straight stitch, zigzag stitch, satin stitch, pattern stitch, or couching.
Technique:	Fabric shapes can be cut first and then stitched to background, or stitched to background first and then trimmed. Use the second technique for appliqué on toweling. Fabric shapes can be held in place by using hands, pinning, taping, basting, or attaching with an iron-on product.
Suggested fabrics:	*Net* used over other fabrics can soften color and design and can create a shadow effect. It can be embroidered first.
	Cotton gauze gives lively contrast to matte fabrics like felt and organdy. It can also be embroidered first.
	Felt does not fray, and comes in wonderful colors.
	Metallic fabric glints through net or gauze.
	Fabrics with rich designs can be good for background or appliqué shapes or both.
	Textured silks, velvets, wools, brocades, etc. add interest.
	Contrasting fabrics, as rough with shiny, are also interesting.
	Patterned weaves stand out through sheer chiffon.
	Embroidered fabrics can serve as background or appliqué shapes.
	Sheer fabrics can be used for a background on which shapes float.
	Use any fabric your machine will stitch—explore soft leather, gold and silver kid, and plastics.
Hints for success:	Use preshrunk, colorfast, no-iron fabrics if possible; for best results, use backing or a hoop. A puffed look can be pleasing.

Inlaid Appliqué
This is a precision method of cutting shapes and holes in a background to match and stitch together. Use zigzag stitch, satin stitch, pattern stitch, or fagoting. The line of meeting of fabric can be couched over with yarn or cord.

Reverse Appliqué

Fabrics are layered, and a design is created by cutting away shapes rather than adding on. The color below is exposed as top layers are cut. Plan carefully the order of colors according to the size and location of shapes to be cut away. Edges can be finished off as in inlaid appliqué. Appliqué collage technique can be used.

Laid-On Appliqué

Cut pieces from one material, arrange on background, and stitch.

Appliquéd Collage

Place fabric on background and stitch around shape desired. Cut away excess fabric.

Or place both fabrics in hoop and use satin stitch or other appropriate stitch around shape edge; cut away fabric.

Or trace design on wrong side of background fabric with special tracing paper. An iron-on product can be used and traced on; This is good for rough and irregularly woven fabric. Attach material to be appliquéd on right side of background fabric. Place in hoop and straight stitch along traced lines on wrong sides. Turn to right side and remove from hoop. Cut away excess fabric.

Multicolor Appliqué Work

Technique: 1. Tack on only the lower part of the appliqué material. Sew around; where colors overlap use straight stitch. Use zigzag stitch on all other contours (A).

2. Trim away surplus appliqué material, cutting as closely as possible to zigzag stitching. Where a straight stitch has been used leave 1/8 inch beyond stitches (B).

3. When covering the contours leave the straight-stitched edge uncovered. This will be covered by the next part (C). Complete in the usual manner for appliqué work, placing the next piece over the first and covering the edges (D).

4. For several shapes of the same size, cut a cardboard template of the shape. Place on back of fabric, outline with pencil, and cut out. Keep similar shapes separate and unwrinkled in a flat envelope until used.

Appliqué with Couching

See section on couching.

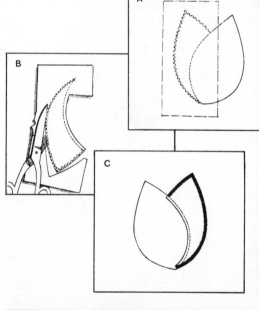

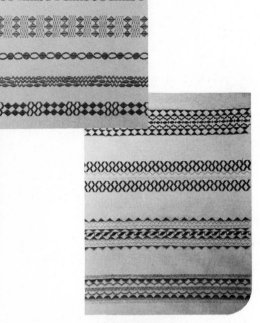

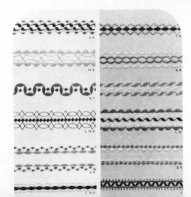

PATTERN STITCHES

Technical Hints:

Sewing over seams: Give fabric a little extra push from the front.

Lining up designs: Use fabric edge or guide presser foot along previous line, or draw a line to follow if necessary, and use edge or center of presser foot for guide.

Buttonholes or buttons: Take into consideration when designing. A pattern does not have to be difficult or complex to be effective; one or two well-chosen pattern lines and colors will do.

Continuous lines of pattern stitches: To make the design match on return when forming a circle, square, etc., a gentle push or pull of the fabric will help.

When beginning pattern stitching, make sure the bobbin is full. This avoids having to match the pattern if bobbin thread runs out.

Fabrics

Different fabrics respond differently to pattern stitches. Some need only to be guided from the side; others need only a gentle pull or push. Still others need to be helped from both sides for smooth stitching. Practice on a scrap. When sewing on knit or tricot, if a garment must stretch—as panties, pants, etc.— keep that in mind when choosing the pattern stitch; experiment first.

Experiment with colors as well as pattern. Try using the same pattern with the same color, and the same pattern with different colors. Stitch lines side by side or make color changes on a continuous line. Try strong value contrasts of the same color, delicate value contrasts of different colors, and anything else you think will work well.

Sewing Technique

• When turning an edge corner, keep needle in fabric, raise presser foot, and turn; check to make sure distance of stitches from the next edge will be the same. Lower presser foot and stitch. Go a little further on first edge, if necessary.

• If you make a mistake or don't like the design, use a seam ripper or embroidery scissors to carefully cut stitches and remove. Work from back of fabric. If you don't want to do this, stitch over pattern with a satin stitch, or try stitching another pattern or several beside the first; try a different color or colors.

• If the pattern-stitched line is a little crooked, a small adjustment can be made by gently pulling the fabric, holding it on both sides of the crooked lines, a little above on one side and a little below on the other.

• If motifs do not match, push the work slightly; this will distort one motif, but the next pattern should match correctly.

• Guide fabric to match motifs—place all fingers on fabric on both sides of stitching. Middle fingers guide the most; they

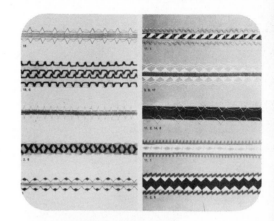

should be exactly beside the pattern or motif being stitched. After a motif has been sewn, the fingers move down to the next one, and so on.

This is necessary only if you want perfect matching. Matching is generally achieved by starting the second row correctly. The density of the first row of stitches may hold back the fabric a little; this can be adjusted somewhat by a gentle pull or push of the fabric for the second row. Practice both methods.

• When combining several pattern rows, if the outer rows match, sew the center row first.

• Fancy or zigzag patterns can be sewed over braid. First baste the braid on straight, then sew pattern stitches over it.

• Study your machine manual to learn what pattern stitch combinations can be worked with your machine; the possibilities are endless. The illustrations show some of the patterns that can be sewed with the Bernina.

Needles and Threads

Pattern Stitches can be used with double or triple needles. Do a few stitches to determine how wide your needle should swing (stitch width). *See Double Needle section.*

Pattern stitches can be used with fine yarn or embroidery floss in the bobbin and worked from the reverse side. For a napped look, carefully pick the stitches with a seam ripper.

The various pattern stitches can also be used with surface couching; *see section on Couching.*

Design Possibilities

Pattern stitches can be used to embroider flowers and other designs. To pattern stitch flowers on chiffon,

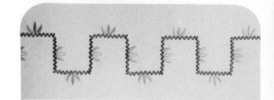

1. Use hoop and typing paper underneath for chiffon.

2. Start design on scraps to get beginning of pattern—pattern indicator is a big help.

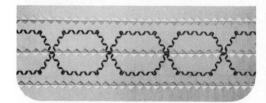

3. Watch through presser foot as you work to stop stitching at the desired part of the pattern. A good stitch indicator is helpful here.

4. Check stretch of fabric in hoop to be certain it is tight for *each* petal, leaf, etc. of design.

COUCHING

Couching is a technique of fastening a thread or threads to the surface of a fabric with stitches or groups of stitches; usually the fastening threads are thinner than the thread being attached. This technique can be used with embroidery floss, cord, all weights and types of yarn, Lurex, strips of felt, leather, fabric, and plastic —anything stitchable. Unstitchables like beads can be strung and couched. Any fabric can be used, from net to silk, chiffon to fur, homespun to vinyl.

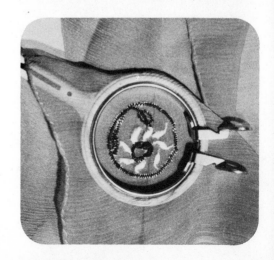

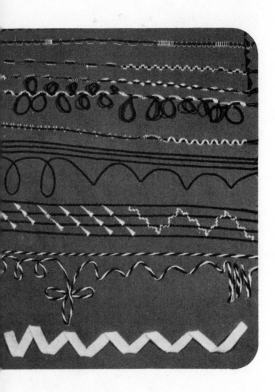

Surface Couching

When using embroidery floss or fine wool, follow this procedure:

• Remove labels.

• Open skein to avoid tangling.

• For couching small length of floss, cut floss; for couching long length, hang opened skein on machine's second spool holder or hold it carefully in right hand for working ease.

• Put end of floss through hole in embroidery foot, front to back, or place under embroidery foot.

• Center floss between toes and guide it carefully, front to back. Unwind as needed.

The illustration shows several examples of surface couching.

Row 1:   Single couched floss with zigzag and varied stitch lengths, open pattern stitch.

Row 2:   Same as Row 1, right side more closed pattern stitch.

Row 3:   Same as Row 2; pattern stitch goes above and below couched line.

Row 4:   Loops with patterns, or with zigzag stitch:

a. Embroider one pattern as floss is couched.

b. Hold fabric down firmly and raise presser foot; needle can be up or down.

c. Pull out floss to form loop in front of stitched pattern.

d. Lower foot and continue pattern; repeat looping as much as desired. Notice that loops can be on both sides of pattern, depending on stitch used, and of various sizes.

e. Experiment with various patterns. A simpler version can be done with zigzag stitch, satin stitch, or varied stitch width satin stitch.

Row 5:   Variations of rows 1 and 2.

Row 6:   Simple parallel lines of couched floss.

Row 7:   Loops formed with couched floss.

a. Gently turn fabric while stitching.

b. At end of loop, with needle in fabric, raise presser foot, turn, lower, and stitch; repeat until loop is completed.

c. Check floss after each turn before stitching to be sure it is flat; pull gently if necessary.

d. For a pointed curve, stitch to point. Leave needle in fabric, raise presser foot, make a sharp turn, and lower presser foot; stitch. For precision, draw a line in pencil on fabric and follow it slowly.

Row 8: Pattern stitch can cross several rows of couching; the lines of either need not be straight. It can be controlled to correspond to rows by gently pulling from front to back.

Row 9: Two colors or tones of embroidery floss can be twisted together and stitched down with nylon thread, using zigzag stitch, stitch width 3 and stitch length 2; or the thread can be a contrasting color in zigzag or pattern stitch.

Row 10: A strip of felt is couched with floating couching satin stitch method.

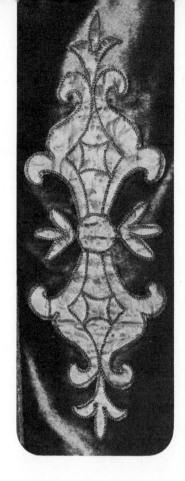

Surface couching worked from reverse.

Shown is a detail of *From the Walls of Kings.* It is couched with red spool thread and gold Lurex (on bobbin) on gold fabric with a red velvet background; the straight stitch is used. If fabric is stitched down with straight stitch on the right side, it is easy to follow the line on the reverse side when couching.

Surface couching with heavier yarns.

Technique: 1. Place heavier yarn through opening in presser foot for needle.

2. Yarn is threaded from above and out the back for ease of handling.

3. If short length of yarn, cut; if long, place ball in shopping bag hung from chair back.

4. Stitch a few times to secure yarn end and stitch. Yarn is easy to guide and flows quickly.

The illustration shows several examples of work done this way.

Row 1: Free-surface machine embroidery with visible zigzag. For least visibility, thread can be invisible nylon in spool and same color as fabric in bobbin.

Row 2: Free-surface machine embroidery with invisible zigzag. Outside yarn silk bouclé, inside yarn mohair loop. Contrasting yarn textures and values can add interest.

Row 3: Free-surface machine embroidery; at left, visible zigzag, at right, invisible zigzag. Very bulky yarn was couched, and the first half of both left and right designs was then fluffed with a seam ripper for a tufted look.

Row 4: Double-needle work; one needle couched and the other created a stitched line beside the

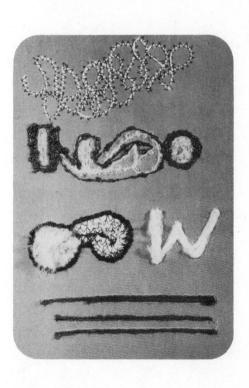

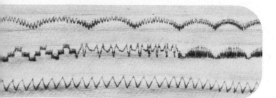

yarn. At end of top row, fabric was turned and another close row stitched.

Relief couching.

Floss or yarn can also be placed under the fabric and couched to give a relief effect to the stitches on the right side. A pattern stitch or zigzag stitch can be used.

Couching from Reverse

With this method, floss, fine wool, or Lurex is hand-wound on a bobbin and stitching worked from the reverse side. Several stitch techniques can be used.

Zigzag stitch can be used with varying stitch widths, straight stitch with varying stitch lengths. Free ends of floss can be used for fringe or tassels or left at intervals between bands of stitches. Couching from reverse can also be combined with free-surface machine embroidery to draw anything freely, and satin stitch and pattern stitches can be given a relief effect by couching from reverse. Remember, as you are working from the reverse side, embroidery floss ends will be on the right side. They can be threaded in a large-eyed needle and pulled through to the back if desired; don't clip them too close or they'll come back up.

Floating Couching

Floating couching is done with transparent nylon thread in the needle and thread the color of the fabric on the bobbin. The thread seems to disappear, making the couched patterns seem to float on the background fabric. The pattern is attached at a minimum of points.

This detail from a skating skirt shows floating couching with the satin stitch, used in the large flower, leaves, and stem. The three smaller flowers were couched with straight stitch.

This motif figure, a detail from a Hungarian blouse, was worked in reverse couching with straight stitch for the lines. Satin stitch was used for the leaves and flowers.

Floating couching also has a wide potential for loosely attached flowers and other designs. As shown in the illustrations, petals are made by stitching the floss or yarn only at the ends, with the petal shape itself left free. Borders, flower centers, and tufted effects can be worked with straight-stitched lines, loops, twists, French knots, spirals, and any other technique that appeals. Stitching is indicated by dotted lines, yarn by solid lines.

This sampler shows a variety of floating couching techniques, satin and straight stitches and several twists and spirals.

CUT WORK

This technique, whose name is sometimes also given to open-space stitching, can produce a wide variety of effects. It is used with layers of fabric, the top layer being cut away, or on a single layer. The open area can be outlined with pattern stitches or stitched across as

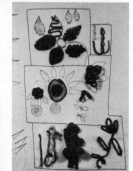

in open-space stitching. Any fabric combination is acceptable—silk and burlap, burlap and velvet, or anything that appeals. The results can range from delicate to rustic to elegant.

Technique: 1. Draw a shape (petal, etc.) on fabric, or on two layers of fabric.

2. Stretch tightly in hoop.

3. Straight stitch around outline several times.

4. Cut away inside shape on single fabric or top fabric.

5. Zigzag stitch around edge; allow needle to overlap cut area.

6. If desired, stitch across open area.

QUILTING

Quilting is a technique used to join two layers of fabric, usually with a batting between them, with rows or patterns of stitches. *Italian quilting* forms narrow channels with rows of stitching and accentuates them with pulled-through cording; *trapunto* is relief quilting formed by stuffing certain areas of the pattern.

Italian Quilting

Technique: 1. Stitch double fabric or lined fabric in rows about 1/8 inch apart to form channels.

2. With large-eyed semiblunt needle, pull yarn or cord through channels. For curves, needle goes out in back and returns. To keep yarn in place on sharper curves, catch a bit of fabric with needle before returning.

3. Pull end of yarn out in back when finished.

4. Tack down or tie ends.

Trapunto

Technique: 1. Two layers of fabric are stitched through to form area for quilting. The bottom fabric should be fairly stiff, the upper fabric soft and pliable.

2. Make a small slit in the back of the area to be stuffed.

3. Stuff the enclosed area with Dacron, cotton, nylon stockings, scraps, etc.

4. Stitch the slit together.

DOUBLE-NEEDLE STITCHING

Double-needle stitching—a triple needle is also available—is used for pin tucks and for decorative couching from reverse. Pin tucks on

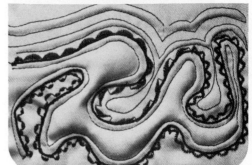

fine fabrics are a classic decoration. Always use fine thread, the same color as the fabric—No. 60 for natural fibers, No. 120 metrosene for polyester fabric.

Suggested fabrics: Soft, even-weave materials: solid-color jersey, double-knits, wool, muslin, velvet, organza, etc.

Technique: 1. Use single fabric with no paper underneath.

2. Sew pin tucks.

3. Iron with damp cloth. Fabric can now be cut for assembling garment.

Presser Foot	Needle	Fabric
9 grooves *or* zigzag foot	1.8 mm	*Very fine.* Do not use fancy stitched fabrics; they lack body. Do not use embroidery floss or cord underneath. Mostly sewn on one presser foot width.
7 grooves	2 mm	*Fine fabrics.* Pearl cotton for fancy stitches. One or two needles. Use exactly one presser foot width.
5 grooves	3 mm	*Medium fabrics.* Use embroidery floss or cord; fancy stitches can be close to tucks but not between needles.
3 grooves	4 mm	*Heavy fabric.* Use heavier cord and fancy stitches, as for medium fabric.

Double Fabric

Double fabric is used only for hems on sleeves, dresses, tablecloths, sheets; or facings on blouse fronts or neck sections.

Technique: Sew from top with a double needle. The fabric is raised less than single fabric, but the process gives a pin-tucked effect and hems at the same time. For heavier fabric, thread the bobbin case and close top tension a fraction.

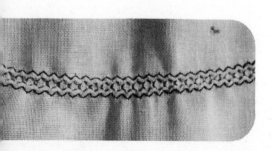

Pin tucks are also pretty sewn in squares, circles, or wavy lines, or on very fine fabrics with a shadow effect. Use a double hemstitch needle with zigzag stitch; the illustrated trim was worked at stitch width 1¾, stitch length 1¾.

To sew corners,

1. Leave needle in fabric.

2. Lift presser foot.

3. Half turn work and lower presser foot.

4. With needle in fabric, turn hand wheel for stitch.

5. Lift presser foot and complete the turn.

6. Lower presser foot and continue sewing.

Use pin-tuck foot and double needle for designs sewn in between or close to tucks, as shown here. To do double-needle embroidery without pin tucks, use embroidery foot.

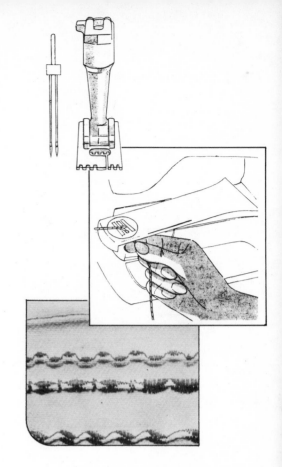

Double-Needle Couching

Work from reverse side with embroidery floss, cord, or yarn. An embossed effect results on right side. Stitch a few times to secure floss after it is threaded through needle plate or placed under fabric and under presser foot. Hold some in right hand, being careful not to tangle it; cut if only a short length is needed.

> Row 1: Straight stitch.
>
> Rows 2,3,4: Pattern stitches.

If thread breaks, test the pattern on another fabric to get the same place in the pattern; rethread and continue stitching.

If needle plate hole is not used, be careful that embroidery floss end does not get stitched down in pattern.

If it tangles or for some reason must be cut, begin with it again, leaving a little extra as at the start of the row. Cut extra floss later, close to fabric, and glue down with any waterproof glue; use very little glue. Stitch a few times to secure at ends of row.

HEMSTITCHING (TRELLIS WORK)

Use embroidery foot and single hemstitch needle. For fine fabrics, use zigzag, stitch width 2, stitch length l. Trellis work with metallic thread, Lurex, can be used as a border; the thread is led through the hole in the embroidery foot and couched on.

> Technique: 1. Sew first row of stitching.
>
> 2. Leave tip of needle in work; turn.
>
> 3. Sew second row. Needle will pierce holes of first row on one side.

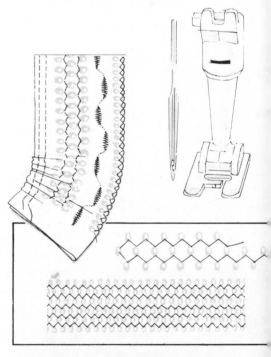

Ruche

> Technique: 1. Iron bias strip of organdy in two.
>
> 2. Sew hemstitches at desired distance over folded edge.
>
> 3. Sew ornamental stitch in between with a normal needle.
>
> 4. An entire insertion is worked in the same way.

Trellis Work Appliqué

> Technique: 1. Hem stitch a piece of fine material as described until you get a trellis effect.
>
> 2. With this trellis make a normal appliqué.
>
> 3. Finish by cutting away background material under trellis.

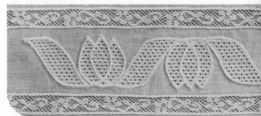

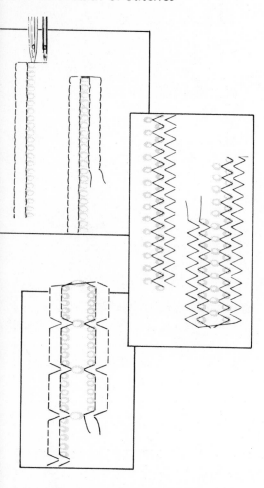

Double Hemstitch Needle

Technique: 1. Using regular sewing foot, zigzag stitch width 0, stitch length 1¾, sew first hemstitch row of embroidery.

2. Raise needle and foot; turn work.

3. Put wide needle into first hole of previously sewn row and continue sewing. Do not hold back work.

Zigzag hemstitching.
Use zigzag stitch width 1¾, length 1¾.

Technique: 1. Sew the first side of the hemstitch row.

2. Just pierce the last *left* stitch.

3. Turn hand wheel back again; raise presser foot and turn work.

4. With wide needle, stitch through the previously pierced hole and continue sewing. Do not hold the fabric back.

Fancy Hemstitching.
Use zigzag stitch width 1¾, stitch length 1¾.

Technique: Work as for zigzag hemstitching. Blind stitch is shown; any pattern stitch can be used. Below are examples of hemstitching with a napped pattern stitch (threads picked with seam ripper) and fancy hemstitching.

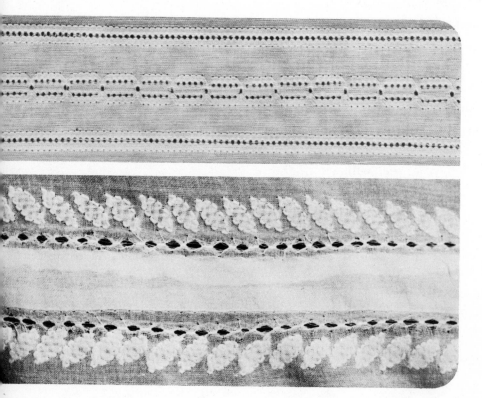

ENGLISH EYELET

Special attachments are needed for this work, but it's worth the trouble. You'll need:

- Eyelet embroidery foot
- Special plate
- slide ⎫
- slide ⎬ 2 sizes
- Round awl
- Square awl

Use zigzag stitch width 1½ (small) or 2½ (large), needle position left.

Preparation

1. Set machine. Change needle plate, placing screw at top left, or correct preparation for your machine.

2. Loosen screw; secure—requires slide with prong slot on the left. Do not tighten screw yet.

3. Place the needle, swinging to the right, into the opening. Then slide the plate along until the needle is just inside the prong. Carefully tighten the screw.

Technique: 1. Always use hoop; stretch material.

2. Punch holes with hand awl, pushing halfway through for small and through for large eyelets. Square awl is for felt and leather.

3. Secure work onto prong and sew eyelet embroidery. Sew twice around small holes and three times around large.

4. Important: Turn the frame faster for the first round than for the following rounds. Do not change sewing speed. Turn work without stopping or varying movement; find a comfortable way to hold it. When sewing with large pieces of material —fold back the corners and secure them with pins to prevent pulling when turning. Start turning as soon as machine is in motion, and stop machine as soon as turning is finished; otherwise eyelet will be uneven.

5. Set zigzag to stitch width 0. Turn work again and fasten with a few stitches.

Ornamental Stitching around Eyelet

Work with a hoop. Set machine for zigzag stitch width 4, stitch length 0, any stitch pattern you desire. Put needle into its highest position; loosen screw and move slide toward the left according to size of circle required. The opening in the plate underneath should be clear and not covered by the slide.

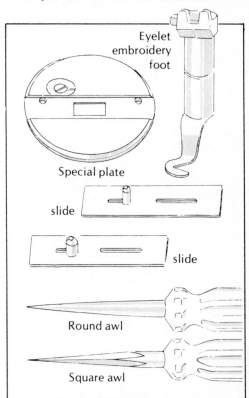

Eyelet embroidery foot

Special plate

slide

slide

Round awl

Square awl

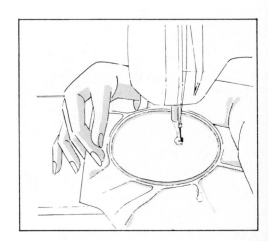

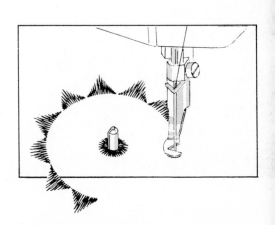

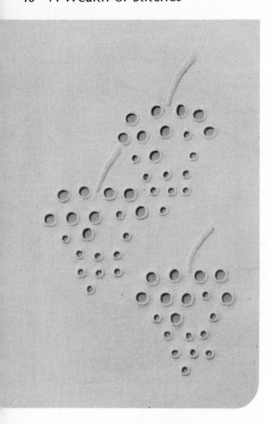

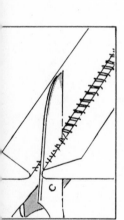

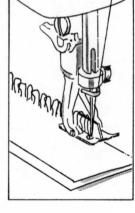

Technique: 1. Secure embroidered hole onto the prong; set pattern indicator to center and embroider circle.

2. As the drop feed control is lowered, the embroidery hoop must be turned by hand.

3. The circle cannot be sewn in one motion; sew as with punch embroidery.

4. Interrupt the work after a few motifs and renew hold on embroidery hoop.

5. For neat and even work sew *slowly* and *evenly*.

Eyelets can be worked first with an open zigzag stitch as a padding for a satin stitch. Holes can be enlarged, or can be grouped for texture. They can also be backed with other fabrics for contrast.

CIRCULAR EMBROIDERY

This technique requires special attachments. A good machine allows for a variety of approaches to circular embroidery. Material should be stiffened with an iron-on product or, better, worked in a hoop. Some fabrics may require both.

TAILOR TACKING, FRINGING, AND FAGOTING

Tailor Tacking

Technique: 1. Set zigzag; put needle in its highest position to avoid damage. Attach special tailor tack presser foot.

2. Loosen top tension or remove thread from tension slot. When finished tailor tacking, tighten tension or replace thread in tension slot.

3. Draw thread to the rear under presser foot. Lay thread sideways before starting to sew.

4. Transfer pattern to fabric with tailor's chalk; pin before basting to prevent slipping.

5. Stitch to transfer pattern onto fabric; tailor tacking foot forms loops.

6. Pull both sides of material apart gently and cut through the threads.

Fringing

Use zigzag stitch width 4, stitch length about 1. Follow procedure above, 1 through 5; leave loops to form fringe. Many rows of loops, side by side, form a rich texture. The fabric can be gently turned while stitching for curved lines. Back after stitching with an iron-on product to secure.

An interesting texture can also be achieved by clipping the loops after the fabric has been backed with an iron-on product. Stitch loops more closely for greater textural density.

Fagoting

Follow the procedure for tailor tacking; separate fabric layers but do not cut the threads. Another way to achieve fagoting is this technique:

1. Pull through as many threads as you like, depending on kind of material. Stretch work tightly in a hoop. Threads must be straight, otherwise fagoting will be distorted.

2. Set bottom tension very strong, upper tension regular. Thread through extra guide of bobbin case.

3. For thread use No. 50 embroidery thread or No. 100 darning thread; bottom thread can be heavier. For sheets, use sewing thread.

4. Lower feed dog. No presser foot is used.

5. Zigzag width depends on how many threads you want to bind together, and in what kind of material; 2 is about right.

6. Hold hoop as for darning, elbows leaning on table. *Do not forget to lower presser bar.*

7. Sew a few stitches in the material to bind up threads; with zigzag set about 2, four to five threads will be caught. Move hoop slowly over those threads until you reach the other end of the bar, doing the last stitches by hand. Make the last on the right side, leaving needle down.

8. Set zigzag on 0. Make a stitch in the edge and one back; move the third stitch, catching the new threads, the fifth stitch in the edge again and back, about two threads deep.

9. While the needle is still down, set on zigzag again to start the next bar. Always make the beginning and end of each bar moving the balance wheel by hand. If the needle comes down to the wrong side, move the hoop until the needle is in the right place.

10. If the bar keeps moving while you sew, the material has loosened itself; you must restretch it. The success of this embroidery depends on well-stretched material and correct holding of the hoop.

Drawn thread work.

This is another method of fagoting.

Technique: 1. Any open-weave fabric can be used; some warp and/or weft threads can be removed to create patterns.

2. Use free-surface machine embroidery, tensions normal to tight.

3. Set machine on zigzag; stitch length and width can vary for different effects.

4. Stitch down opened areas. Threads will be caught together, resulting in an almost lacy look.

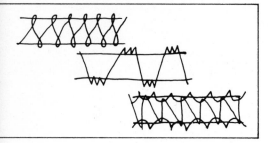

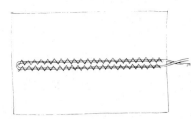

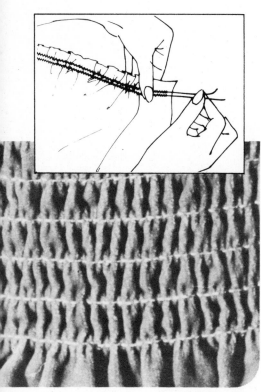

Fagoting in a hoop.

Fagoting can also be done with this technique:

1. Place two pieces of fabric in hoop with a space between their edges.

2. Use open-space stitching to create fagoting.

Surface or floating couching can be used, individually or together, to achieve a variety of line designs.

SMOCKING AND GATHERING

Technique: 1. Thread pearl cord through hole in embroidery foot from front to back; hold in place under presser foot if you do not have this convenience.

2. Oversew with zigzag, stitch width 2, stitch length 2. The stitching will not touch the cord.

3. Pull cord to gather; secure with two or three stitches. If using elastic cord, pull while sewing first row. Pull material while sewing other rows.

4. Pull cord ends to back and tie to fasten. Repeat with several lines for smocking, pulling cords after stitching.

5. Pattern stitches can be embroidered over lines for more decorative effect.

Sheer or short pieces of fabric can be gathered by straight stitch, stitch length 4—sew two rows and then hold both bottom threads and gather up to width desired. Parallel rows of zigzag stitch on soft pliable fabric, without hoop or backing, give a smocked effect.

ENLARGING AND REDUCING DESIGNS

Designs can be enlarged or reduced with this simple technique. Begin with simple designs; as you gain confidence, go on to more complex patterns. You'll need tracing and typing or wrapping paper, a sharp pencil, a ruler, and tape.

Technique: 1. Trace design or motif onto tracing paper; tape tracing paper and design, if necessary.

2. Determine the final size and choose a size scale. If a ¼-inch section is to be enlarged to one inch, the scale is 4 to 1. If it is to be enlarged to ½ inch, the scale is 2 to 1. The procedure is reversed for reductions.

3. Use ruler to make two grids, one with ¼-inch squares on tracing paper and one with one-inch

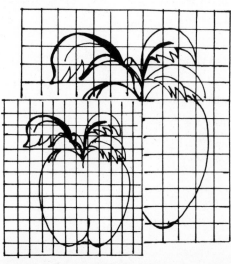

squares on typing or wrapping paper. If you wish, number the squares, vertically and horizontally. The numbers on the small grid should correspond to those on the large grid.

4. Place the tracing paper with the smaller grid over the tracing of the design. Tape in place.

5. Draw all lines of the motif or design.

6. On large grid squares, fill in all lines to correspond to those in smaller grid squares. Smooth lines to finish enlargement, making any corrections you feel necessary. The enlarged design does not have to be exact; designs can be used from the grid or traced off if desired. Enlargements can be used many times.

7. Transfer design to fabric.

TRANSFERRING DESIGNS

REVERSE TRACING

1. On *back* of tracing paper, if the design has been traced directly or enlarged, go over lines of design with a soft pencil.

2. Pin or tape design right-side-up on fabric.

3. Retrace lines with a harder pencil. Lines of the design should appear on fabric.

DRESSMAKERS' CARBON PAPER

1. Place carbon paper between design and fabric; tape all three in place.

2. Retrace lines of design with hard pencil; lines should appear on fabric.

Dressmakers' carbon paper is preferable to pencil tracing because it creates fewer smudges on fabric. It comes in light colors, for use on dark fabrics, and dark colors, for use on light fabrics.

TRANSFER PATTERNS

Many beautiful designs are available from pattern companies; these can be easily ironed on. Embroidery kits can also be adapted to machine embroidery.

I. Secure fabric on ironing board with pins or tape; a smooth fabric will give the best results.

2. Secure pattern, ink side down, on fabric.

3. Iron should not be too hot; low or rayon setting is usually correct.

4. Do not glide iron. Lift up and down firmly on pattern.

5. Before removing iron-on pattern, check to be sure transfer is complete.

6. Now glide warm iron over surface and lift the paper away from fabric quickly.

7. Save iron-on patterns; they may be reusable.

COPYING OR HOT-IRON PENCIL

1. Trace design with copying or hot-iron pencil onto typing paper (be sure point is sharp).

2. Erase all mistakes with ink eraser before transferring; pencil dye is difficult to remove from fabric.

3. Now transfer design as you would transfer any iron-on pattern.

4. Save pattern; it is often reusable.

IRON-ON PELLON

1. Transfer embroidered design onto Pellon.

2. Press it onto wrong side of fabric.

3. Sew through lines of design with free-surface machine embroidery or straight stitch.

4. Embroider on right side, or, if technique used requires it, from reverse.

5. Pellon can be steamed off later, if desired.

DIRECT TRACING

Direct tracing can be used when fabric is transparent or semitransparent.

1. Place design under fabric.

2. Trace lines with soft pencil or tailor's chalk.

TACKING

When fabric is coarse or very highly textured, tacking is often the best way to transfer a design.

1. Trace design onto tracing paper.

2. Tack, tape, or pin paper to fabric.

3. Baste over design lines. Carefully tear paper away.

STRAIGHT STITCHING WITH MACHINE

Designs in newspapers and magazines and other same-size patterns can be quickly and easily transferred this way. This is a good process for monograms.

1. Tape, pin, or hold tracing on fabric.

2. Straight stitch over lines with machine.

3. Tear paper away carefully.

BLOCKING EMBROIDERY

Finished embroidery is sometimes puckered or curled at the edges. When this is the case, blocking may be necessary.

Technique: 1. Wet embroidered object thoroughly. Use cold water to minimize chance of colors running.

2. Pin to a strong cardboard backing to stretch well. Pin center of each edge first, working outward so entire piece is fully stretched.

3. Let dry thoroughly, overnight.

TECHNICAL EMBROIDERY HINTS

1. Pull bobbin thread up through cloth.

2. Threads should be placed through toes of presser foot and behind it; otherwise they will become tangled with embroidery stitches.

3. Always cut threads on top as close as possible after the first couple of stitches to avoid embroidering over them.

4. Check tension; stitches should look the same on both sides.

5. Always turn work with needle in the fabric.

6. Lift presser foot only if necessary; this is the case for a wide turn.

7. Keep stitch length even.

8. Different length stitches give quite different effects. A short stitch, about ½, gives a finely stitched look. A long stitch, about 2½, makes it possible to work with greater facility and speed.

9. Let the feed dog move the fabric when it is in use.

10. Gently guide the fabric from the left side. If you push or pull, the stitch will be irregular and the needle may bend or break.

11. Use a scrap of the material you're working on to test the pattern.

12. Be sure machine is positioned at the beginning of the pattern if you are using automatic stitches.

13. To take work off the machine, pull it backwards, not forward.

14. Choose the proper needle for the thread in use. See needle-thread chart on page **16.**

15. If a loop on top of fabric is desired, keep upper tension loose. If a loop on reverse side is desired, keep bobbin tension loose. This irregularity can be an advantage in machine embroidery; if tension is too tight, thread breaks.

16. Presser foot lever should always be down when embroidering so thread tension is maintained.

chapter 5

fabrics

In your experiments so far you may have used a variety of fabric weights and textures. In that case, you are already aware of the fact that different fabrics respond differently to machine embroidery. If you have not yet become familiar with the different responses of various fabrics, this is the time to experiment further.

You can try these experiments as you use certain fabrics. Or you can try them all at once, producing your own visual catalog of how the various fabrics react. This has several advantages: having your fabric catalog at your disposal is both inspirational and practical. It will help you choose fabrics that are best suited to the type of machine embroidery you plan to do. You'll know what fabric to buy, and you won't have to practice with your fabric every time you embroider.

From experimenting on gauze fabric, for example, you will see its great possibilities for open work—airy blouses, summer dresses, curtains, and anything else that lends itself well to open laciness. If you want a crisp, clear pattern of embroidery on a guest towel, a place mat, or anything else, you'll know that fabric that has a firmer surface is preferable. For this application, cottons, synthetics, silk, wool, and linen or linenlike polyester or rayon fabrics are excellent. Crispness can also be achieved on a great variety of other fabrics with the help of stiffeners—spray starch, typing paper, or iron-on Vilene or Pellon. The pucker of smocking, or the relief effect of embossed fabrics, are easy to achieve, too—and your experiments will show you how the softer silklike rayon fabrics can produce these delightful effects, quickly and easily.

The charts in this section are a guide for what you can expect in your experiments, a fun way to take the guesswork out of choosing fabrics. And a note on the care of embroidered fabrics will help you keep your embroideries looking their best long after the final stitches are made.

AN EXPERIMENTAL CATALOG

To put together your experimental swatch catalog, assemble six-by-eight-inch swatches of various fabrics, choosing from what you have on hand and from the fabrics listed in this section—try to choose at

THE JOY OF MACHINE EMBROIDERY

least two fabrics of each type. Keep a notebook and pencil handy to record your results.

Assemble spray starch, typing paper, and iron-on Vilene or Pellon. A variety of these tried on different fabrics will increase your understanding of how they react to various machine embroidery techniques.

Prepare the fabric:

    1. With a pencil, divide the back of each swatch into four horizontal sections.

    2. Spray one area of each swatch with spray starch.

    3. On the second section, attach a piece of typing paper on the back of the fabric; pin or baste on.

    4. Iron the Vilene or Pellon on the third section.

    5. Leave the fourth section plain.

Now start your experiments. On each swatch of fabric sew a row each of satin stitch, zigzag stitch, and automatic pattern stitch, if possible. The stitch rows should cross all four prepared sections. When you reach the bottom of each row of stitches, gently turn the fabric and continue to stitch slowly. This will help you see the reaction of the fabric to turning motions. Sometimes puckering or embossing will result, and as you will see, this can be very useful.

FABRIC TYPES

Weight	Examples
Very sheer	Chiffon, net, georgette, silk, organza, ninon
Sheer	Organdy, voile, marquisette, thin silk, fine silk, gauze, voile, net
Lightweight	Lawn, dotted swiss, muslin, tricot, linen, crepe, wool challis
Medium	denim, wool, felt, burlap, taffeta, crepe, linen, velvet, garbardine, chintz
Medium heavy	Sailcloth, corduroy, madras, wool, flannel
Heavy	Duck, wool, damask, leather, fleece, velveteen, brocade
Very heavy	Hessian canvas, wool, plastic, tapestry, fur
Knits, single and double	Natural wool, cotton; synthetics

FABRIC FINISHES

Also of interest to the machine embroiderer are the various fabric finishes. Besides the common stain-resistant treatment, fabrics may also be:

- *embossed*, with a raised design.
- *napped*, with a fluffy look.
- *sueded*, to resemble leather suede.
- *mercerized*, to add luster, strength, and elasticity.

SPECIAL CARE OF EMBROIDERY

1. Follow cleaning recommendations for specific material.

2. Use steam iron on back with a soft pad underneath, or

3. Stretch over damp white blotter until dry if design includes a heavy raised surface, beads, or buttons.

4. If care is taken while embroidering, little or no stretching is necessary later.

TEXTURE AND PATTERN

Any fabric can serve as a background for machine embroidery as long as its texture and pattern do not conflict with the stitches being worked. An actively structured weave or a heavy fabric may mask the stitches unnecessarily and keep embroidery from standing out. On the other hand, a thick velvet or mohair fabric can give an interesting look when it is machine embroidered. And a complicated weave structure or a heavy texture can enhance your work when the material is couched with cords, yarns, or metallic threads.

Patterned fabrics can be a real joy to work with if you choose patterns that will be enhanced by embroidered outlines or counterdesigns. They can also be appliquéd onto other backgrounds as ornaments, pockets, or borders. Stripes can be especially fun to embroider over. Striped and plaid fabrics are easier to work with if they are woven rather than simply printed; woven designs help guide the sewing machine.

EFFECTS OF MACHINE EMBROIDERY ON FABRICS

Fabric	Effects of Embroidery
Organdy	Tight tension distorts fabric, causing it to catch light. Use thick thread for crisp line.
Burlap	With thin thread, line is almost lost. With tight tension, zigzag stitch pulls thread for an interesting effect. Fabric threads are easy to cut or pull from design.

Other loose wovens: gauze, lawn, linen, scrim	Crisp clear patterns.
Soft fabrics (without backing): cottons, silks, some rayons, sheerer wools, some synthetics	Stitching puckers fabric to resemble smocking, and can create embossing for relief effect.
Thick fabrics: velvet, mohair, fleece	Embroidery gives a cut look or three-dimensional look; fine stitches disappear.
Patterned fabrics: flowered chintz, abstracts, tie-dyes	Outline emphasizes or joins selected areas; can be combined with cut work or used as background.
Stripes	Can be outlined, worked with cross-over designs, or used as background.
Brocades and large designs	Excellent for trapunto.
Net	Does not fray; stitching edges not necessary. Stitches can almost disappear, can give a shadow effect, can be direct and firm, or can have an uneven appearance with even tension. Both needle and bobbin thread show.
Textured fabrics	With delicate stitches only color and sheen will show. For greater effectiveness with satin stitch, stitch broad bands several times.
Tufted fabrics: terrycloth, pile	Strengthen stitch for more visibility.
Plush, long pile	Stitching alters the direction of the pile.
Plain	The fabric can become the design by using satin stitch fill-in technique around the design area.
Slubbed fabrics	For interesting flecked effect, stitch with strong tone and color contrasts.
Felt	Does not fray; quilts if embroidered when edges are left unstitched. No competing weave, so full richness of design is possible.
Silk twill	Sharp tonal contrasts—threads reflect less than fabric.
Satin weave	High reflective quality, smooth and rich, contrasts well with an agitated matte stitch.

Matte-finish fabrics   Sheen of machine-embroidering cotton stands out in relief.

Coarse fabrics   Heavy embroidering is more pleasing with a strong design.

FABRIC AND DESIGN

1. Different qualities of line can be achieved by altering thread tension or by changing the type of fabric used.

2. Soft fabrics can be worked with crisp, clear embroidery designs, if fabric is not too thick, if stiffening is used.

3. The same weave in different fibers looks different; different weaves in the same fiber look different.

4. A dark line of stitching on a light fabric looks less agitated than the reverse.

5. Delicate fabrics are generally worked with delicate embroidery, but a rich, heavy approach can be surprisingly beautiful.

6. Conversely, heavy fabrics can be treated effectively with delicate embroidering.

7. Light affects different fabrics differently. This difference can be used to advantage on fabrics like satin, some silks, velvets, and brocades.

8. Although most embroidering work is on flat fabric, don't overlook the possibilities of fabrics that have been rolled, twisted, torn, frayed, cut into, and painted on.

SOME COMMON FABRICS

Imported fabrics, although more expensive, are worth exploring once you become more familiar with the rich possibilities of machine embroidery. France is known for its *haute couture,* and produces high-fashion-type natural-fiber fabrics. Switzerland specializes in sheers and cottons, Ireland and Belgium in pure linen, Great Britain in woolens. Japan produces a wide variety of not too expensive specialty brocades; Germany is excellent for synthetics—nylons, polyesters, and so on. And in the future, China should prove a rich source of silks.

The United States has a wide selection of fabrics of all types, styles, and prices without the addition of import costs. In synthetics, the man-made fibers, the United States leads the world. Every fabric has a purpose, so choose one that is appropriate for each project.

COTTON

Cotton is an excellent fabric to begin embroidering on, as there are inexpensive cottons for a variety of uses—at least twenty-five kinds, from gingham to organdy to denim. Cotton is also easy to handle and sew.

If it is not sanforized to control shrinkage, be sure to wash cotton fabric before cutting it, and especially before embroidering. Durable-press cottons and polyester blends are especially good to work with, as they require little or no pressing.

WOOL

The two major types of wool are worsted, made of smooth long wool fibers for firmness, and woolens, softer and more yielding. Both respond well to machine embroidery. The wovens and knits found in both categories have as exciting a variety of type as does cotton.

When choosing wool for machine embroidery, be sure it is:

- moth-proofed.
- washable.
- preshrunk. If not preshrunk, ask a dry cleaner to steam press the fabric, or steam-iron it at home (a little difficult to do evenly). Or wet it with water, roll in a towel overnight, hang to dry.

All knits should be laid flat on a table overnight before cutting or embroidering. If you plan to put in a hem with simple sewing or machine embroidery, let the garment hang overnight first.

Use a ballpoint needle to sew with wool. Silk or nylon thread is generally recommended; as mercerized cotton is the first choice for machine embroidery, experiment to see which you prefer. The grain of the material affects the way the fabric takes machine embroidery, and wovens, especially, should be laid out on the grain when cutting. Pull a thread from the width of the fabric at one end as a guide in laying the grain straight.

Steam press seams as you sew, edges closed and then open. This will help you do a professional-looking job and let you work more easily if you embroider over a seam.

When pressing, avoid sharp edges on hems. Press on the wrong side with a damp pressing cloth, and lay a soft cloth underneath.

If you get a spot on something, remove it quickly so as not to mar the work you've done. Depending upon the fabric, use a gentle soap solution, cleaning fluid, talc, commercial spot removers, or dry cleaning. Your work will also profit from this care. Try not to hand-rub machine embroidery, if possible.

SILK

Silks are available in a dazzling array of rich and subtle colors and textures, brocade and chiffon, satin and shantung, taffeta and twill. Each is appropriate for many and diverse purposes. Organza, for example, with its sheer crisp sheen, is equally adaptable to dressy clothes and dressy curtains; machine embroidery shows up wonderfully well. Faille, with its firmness and delicate rib, is beautiful to embroider. Brocade can be an impressive trapunto headboard or a handsome jacket. Examples of all of these projects appear later.

When sewing with silk, use the thinnest pins you can buy. As altering silk also leaves marks, you may wish to cut and fit silk clothing in muslin first. To cut silk, place it between two pieces of tissue paper. Use a hoop for embroidery if the design permits, and back the fabric with typing paper.

When silk becomes soiled, dry clean it quickly; don't try to remove spots. If it's washable, follow the manufacturer's instructions or hand wash. Bleach only white, and then only if necessary; use only peroxide. A few drops of vinegar in the rinse water adds luster.

LINEN

This elegant, cool fabric is now available wrinkle-resistant or durable-press. Linen mixed with synthetic or man-made fibers has the same look, but is not quite as absorbent and cool or as rich in appearance.

Linen or linen-look fabric comes in all weights, and is marvelous for a great variety of uses. Its colors are subtle, tending toward the naturals—a perfect background for embroidery.

Start your exploration of linen with easy-care polyester linen or all-rayon "linen." All-silk "linen," a beautiful nubbly fabric and the most expensive, should be approached only when your skills are sure.

Sewing linen is easy. Use a fine needle, size 11, for lightweights, size 14 for heavier weights. Press out wrinkles before sewing and before embroidering. Seams should be treated as on other fabrics. Remove stains immediately with cold water; glycerine or white vinegar is helpful. Never iron or wash any fabric before removing stains.

RAYON

Rayons, acetates, and Arnel triacetate are a group of cellulosic fabrics. They are generally inexpensive, and are available in a wide range of colors and types. Their excellent draping qualities and shape retention and their rich feel make them highly desirable for embroidering.

Sewing with rayons is generally easy. Use a No. 11 needle for lightweight, a 14 for heavier linenlike fabrics. Nylon thread or mercerized thread is recommended for rayon, silk or nylon thread and a fine needle for acetate, nylon or polyester thread and a fine needle for Arnel knits. Dry clean these fabrics, or follow the manufacturer's instructions. Arnel can be machine washed and tumble dried, but if it's pleated, it retains its shape better when hand washed.

SYNTHETICS

This whole family of fibers is made from oil or coal.

Nylon

Nylon, one of the first of the man-made fibers, is still widely sought after for its many positive qualities: it has greater strength and resistance to abrasion than any other fiber, and low moisture absorption—this makes it easy to wash and dry although it is not too comfortable to wear—and it is lightweight. These qualities, plus the many beautiful colors and patterns in which nylon is available, make it a good choice for machine embroidery—Antron and Qiana nylon are excellent examples. Nylon is colorfast, too, but it picks up color easily from fabrics that bleed, so it must be washed carefully.

Nylon or polyester thread is recommended, with a No. 11 needle; use a ballpoint needle on knits. If puckering is not desirable, guide the fabric with a light, firm touch, at back and front.

When pressing Qiana, use low wool steam setting. On all other nylon fabric, steam press at 275° on the reverse side or use a damp pressing cloth. Let the fabric cool before removing it from the ironing board, and use paper inserts under seam allowances to avoid marking. Wash nylon according to the manufacturer's instructions; spot clean grease and oil stains first. Fabric softener helps reduce static.

Polyester

All-polyester knits, especially double-knits, are the all-time favorites of the travel wardrobe. Polyester is a wrinkle-resistant, resilient wash-and-wear, with all of the positive qualities of nylon. Some polyesters now have a soil-release finish, "Spectron." This is a good thing to look for, as oil and grease stains tend to cling in untreated fabrics.

In blending with other fibers, polyester retains all its advantages; its faults are often eliminated. A 50 percent polyester in heavier blends (with wool) is a good combination; 65 percent polyester in lighter blends with cotton and rayon and close to 100 percent polyester in very lightweight blends like georgettes and chiffons are others to look for.

Everything you use to sew and embroider synthetics should be polyester or nylon: lining, thread, zipper, binding, trim. Preshrink the zipper by immersing it in hot water; dry and press carefully. Use a No. 11 needle for lightweight fabrics, a No. 14 for heavier materials, and a ballpoint needle for knits. Be sure to preshrink knits before cutting or embroidering them, and don't forget to lay them flat overnight. If you use a polyester-rayon blend with more rayon than polyester, treat it as rayon.

Acrylic

Acrylic, another man-made fabric, is a synthetic wool that has just about everything you could want for machine embroidery where woolens—not worsteds—are appropriate. Acrylic is low in cost; it is wash-and-wear, lightweight, and warm. It has resiliency and good shape retention, and takes permanent pleats. It is colorfast, moth-resistant, resistant to sunlight, oil, and chemicals. And it is available in pile and in fleece forms. Both pile and fleece acrylics make beautifully luxurious blankets or coats. Another luxury-type acrylic is DuPont's Normelle, a cashmere-soft featherweight.

Care for acrylics as for all synthetics; sew and embroider with them as with polyester. Treat acrylic knits like nylon knits, and always use nylon thread.

Stretch Fabrics

Stretch fabrics are incredibly versatile, whether natural, synthetic, or a blend. They can have the look and feel and the other properties of the fiber or blend used, and they are practical for many more items—bathing suits, underwear, ski pants, body shirts, sweaters, and more. Machine embroidery enhances them, and, if the stitches are well chosen, stretches right along with the fabric.

Stretch fabrics made with Spandex have the greatest elasticity; only 10 percent Spandex is necessary for good performance. Anidex is next in elasticity, but has an even superior resistance to chemicals. These stretch fabrics are core-spun; a fine filament of the Spandex or Anidex is the core of the finished strand. Stretch nylon and stretch polyester are made by twisting or coiling the filament yarn and setting with heat.

A one-way stretch can be achieved mechanically, with chemicals applied to the fabric; this is inferior in elasticity, but is less expensive. If a project requires only a little elasticity, choose this one-way-stretch fabric and save money. Choose a good quality two-way stretch, though, for active sportswear—test the fabric when you buy to be sure it snaps back immediately and completely. For bathing suits, choose nylon and Spandex stretch tricot. Stretch garments must also be lined with stretch fabric, and the lining must stretch in the same direction as the garment. Also, be sure you don't embroider over the stretch in such a way as to inhibit it. Test your stitches first on scraps of stretch fabric.

For best results with stretch fabrics, try to choose a pattern with as few seams as possible. Lay the fabric on a table overnight, and then cut with very sharp shears. Check your pattern for the stretch direction necessary. Sewing machine tension should be loosened for these fabrics. Try sewing in the direction of the stretch on a scrap before embroidering; if the thread breaks when the fabric is pulled, adjust the tension.

Follow the manufacturer's instructions to wash stretch fabrics. Dry them flat, and iron with a warm iron, making light fast movements in the opposite direction of the stretch.

LEATHER AND IMITATION LEATHER

Any machine that sews through heavy layers of fabric can also be used to embroider leather and its imitations. Use a roller or Teflon presser foot and a special leather needle, or use a No. 14 needle.

PLASTIC AND OTHER SPECIALTY MATERIALS

Sometimes it helps to apply a small amount of sewing machine oil along a design to be stitched in plastic. A special roller foot is available to ensure proper feeding; long stitches are best to avoid damage.

Piles, fleeces, and furs offer their own particular embroidery challenge—use wide, well-defined designs for effective results.

IDENTIFYING FABRICS

With the many new fibers on the market today and the wide range of blends available you may find it useful, especially when buying an unmarked remnant, to know how to determine what fibers a fabric contains.

Here are two simple tests:

	Burn a thread	Break a thread
Cotton	burns quickly, flares up, smells	Ends curl, are dull
Linen	Like paper or wood, light ash	Breaks in a snap—hard ends
Silk	Flame smolders, leaves black ball	Ends are silky
Wool	Slow burner, animal smell, crisp ash.	Fibers pull apart—ends like sheep's wool
Rayon (viscose)	Like cotton and linen; little, if any, ash	Easy to break—wiry ends
Rayon (acetate)	Melts, curled edges	Easy to break—wiry ends
Nylon	Melts, light brown bead; odor similar to burning wax	Fuzzy ends

chapter 6

the compleat wardrobe

Gone is the Age of Conformity; today's clothes are intended to express, above all, individuality. Machine embroidery is the easy way to self-expression; it is also, if you make your own clothes, a real money-saver in acquiring a unique wardrobe. These design suggestions should serve as a springboard for your own ideas.

BELTS, BUCKLES, AND BOOTS

Make belts by folding embroidered fabric around buckram or around an existing belt, or use ready-made belting, sometimes complete with buckle. Stitch, glue, or press (with an iron-on product) the layers together, with seams on the wrong side. The design possibilities for buckles are greater if the buckles are large. However, small, delicately designed buckles can be a good addition to a slim belt. To cover a buckle, cut the fabric a little larger than the buckle itself. Embroider the fabric as desired; then glue it to the buckle with waterproof glue, or use a press-together buckle form.

PATTERN-STITCHED BELT

Stitches: Pattern Stitch used on entire belt.

Technique: Stitch around belt, in vertical or diagonal stripes, or in undulating lines. On a wide belt, stitch shapes—such as circles, triangles or free forms. Contrasting colors and bits of appliqué can be used. All of these approaches can be interchangeably adapted to scarves and hemlines as well as to belts.

Fabric: Anything your machine can take. Any fabric must be stiffened in some way. Use a special needle for leather if necessary.

Design Source: Stitch Catalog.

By Regina Bartley

BOOTS *(see color insert)*

> *Stitches:* Straight stitch, free-surface machine embroidery, couching, pattern stitch.

> *Technique:* Straight stitch, free-surface machine embroidery, and couching used together with gold Lurex in the bobbin and worked from the reverse side. Pattern stitches worked from the right side.

> *Fabric:* Velvet, soft leather, vinyl, patent leather, or any other boot material. If your machine has a free arm you can embroider a wide range of boots; if not, a zippered boot opens flat enough to embroider.

Design Source: Stitch Catalog.

SCARVES

Your embroidery design can be a simple motif, a border, or an all-over design. Don't overlook the exciting possibilities of open work.

ORIENTAL SCARVES

> *Stitches:* Free-surface machine embroidery, couching, straight stitch.

> *Technique:* Free-surface machine embroidery, couching, and straight stitch used to work entire design; gold and silver Lurex and embroidery floss in the bobbin are couched from the reverse side with the straight stitch.

> *Fabric:* Silk, crepe, or synthetics.

Design Source: Near Eastern embroidery and Oriental carpets.

ALL-OVER GEOMETRIC SCARF
Courtesy Sona, New York

> *Stitches:* Pattern stitch, zigzag stitch, satin stitch, straight stitch.

> *Technique:* Any one or all of these stitches can be adapted to this type of all-over geometric design. A design drawn on the scarf first is easier to stitch. Remember to leave the needle down when you turn a corner.

> *Fabric:* Any suitable material. Very soft fabric puckers (which could be desirable) if not backed before stitching. Experiment on a variety of scraps.

> *Variations:* Try organizing the larger shapes in another way—for example, a square within a square or several circles with the straight bands of stitching going different ways in each.

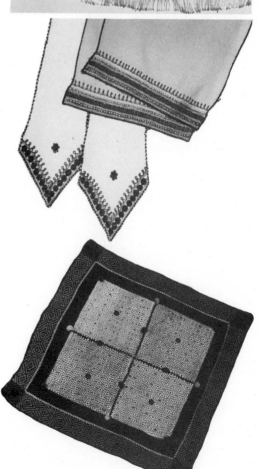

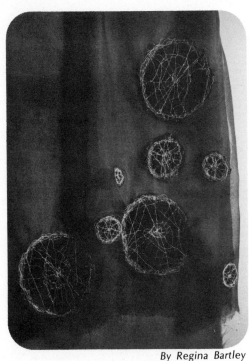

By Regina Bartley

Design Source: This particular scarf is from India. Africa too is a rich source of geometric linear textile design. Go to museums and galleries to observe hard-edge and op art. This type of design is also appropriate for bags, tablecloths, or placemats.

OPEN-SPACE EMBROIDERY SCARF

Stitches: Open-space stitch, straight stitch, appliqué.

Technique: Open-space stitch and straight stitch used to create webs; appliqué used to back webs.

Fabric: Red silk chiffon; backing fabric for webs, darker red velvet.

Variations: This approach can make handsome curtains. Pattern stitches can be used to outline or create designs around webs.

Design Source: Stitch Catalog. Further examples in chapters 14 and 15.

EVENING SCARVES

Stitches: Pattern stitch.

Technique: Embroider a pattern stitch horizontally or diagonally, or let it undulate gently. Choose from the many variations possible.

Fabric: Wool, silk, chiffon, or velvet.

Variation: Try the pattern stitch on a soft bias tape or a silky ribbon, or bordering a band of satin.

Design Source: Stitch Catalog.

EDGED SCARVES

Stitches: Pattern stitch, straight stitch.

Technique: Pattern stitch used for decorative designs; satin stitch used to edge scarves. Do an open satin stitch on the edge and then go over it with a close wide one; be sure to back with typing paper. The satin stitch replaces the rolled hem; any length of fabric can be used.

Fabric: Silk, synthetic, or a soft transparent fabric.

Variations: Pattern stitches can be used in many ways—diagonally, in a herringbone design, vertically, or in a combination of these.

Design Source: Stitch Catalog.

FREE-SURFACE MACHINE EMBROIDERED SCARF

Stitches: Free-surface machine embroidery, straight stitch.

Technique: Free-surface machine embroidery is used, with embroidery floss in the bobbin. The straight stitch is used with spool and bobbin thread of the same color. Technique detailed in Stitch Catalog; *see* section on Free-Surface Machine Embroidery.

Fabric: Net. Be sure to place fabric firmly in a hoop. The same technique can be used on a variety of sheer fabrics; notice the doubled shadow effect of the two overlapping layers.

Design Source: Any line drawing can be used.

FRINGED SCARF

Stitches: Tailor tacking, satin stitch.

Technique: Use the tailor tacking presser foot for fringing the edges or the surface of fabric. Use satin stitch over edge of fringing to outline and secure, first open satin stitch and then a close one for a fine finished look.

Fabric: Silk or synthetic.

Variations: Several rows of fringe can be used; curving lines of fringe are possible. The lines can be secured and outlined with pattern stitches.

Design Source: Stitch Catalog.

By Regina Bartley

HATS

RAIN HAT WITH CHIFFON SCARF

Stitches: Pattern stitch.

Technique: Use pattern stitch in rows encircling hat brim; no backing is necessary. Rows of very open pattern stitch on the scarf can be done without backing for a rich textured effect.

Fabric: For hat, raincoat material; for scarf, silk chiffon.

Variations: For a more dramatic hat, use strong color and tone contrasts or several different colors in the pattern stitches.

Design Source: Stitch Catalog.

By Regina Bartley

CAVALIER CAP
Courtesy Simplicity Pattern Company

Stitches: Pattern stitch, satin stitch.

Technique: Pattern stitch used for inside border lines and design between; satin stitch used for borders. No backing necessary.

Fabric: Felt.

Design Source: Stitch Catalog.

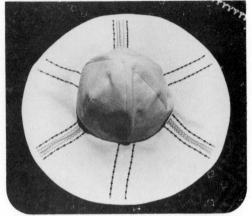

FANCY-BRIMMED HATS
Courtesy Simplicity Pattern Company

Stitches: Pattern stitch, couching.

Technique: Pattern stitch used to make bold spokes on light hat's brim; more subtly, pattern stitch scallops encircle the upper part of the dark hat's brim. Lines of embroidery floss are surface couched on the dark hat with a fine pattern stitch. The hat is green, the machine thread hot pink, and the embroidery floss black. No backing is needed for either hat.

Fabric: Linen or linenlike synthetic.

Design Source: Stitch Catalog.

BAGS

Embroideries can be done separately, cut out, and ironed on. Or embroider fabric first, and then sew the bag together and add handles.

BANANA SPLIT BAG
Courtesy Simplicity Pattern Company

Stitches: Appliqué, satin stitch, pattern stitch.

Technique: Appliqué is used for all shapes. For flat shapes, stitch down first and then cut away excess fabric. Satin stitch used to secure and decorate bowl and bananas; pattern stitch can be used on bananas.

Fabric: Cotton or other suitable fabric.

Design Source: Posters in ice cream parlors; children's books.

PATCHWORK LEATHER BAG

Stitches: Appliqué, straight stitch.

Technique: Shapes of leather are cut and then appliquéd with a simple straight stitch. A special leather needle is used if necessary.

Fabric: Soft leather.

Variations: Bold geometric shapes or strips of leather with a motif on top are handsome. Experiment with the effect of pattern stitches on leather.

Design Source: Wallpapers, cards, children's books.

APPLIQUÉD BAG
Courtesy Simplicity Pattern Company

Stitches: Appliqué, satin stitch, optional pattern stitch.

Technique: Apply appliqué design to bag with iron-on product or stitch on before bag is seamed. Use satin stitch to secure appliqué and for a neat, finished look.

Fabric: Satin and velvet on sailcloth cotton.

Variation: Use pattern stitches to outline and accent shapes effectively.

Design Source: Stylized Egyptian and Grecian drawings of birds and animals; consult your library or museum.

INDIAN BAG
Courtesy Sona, New York

Stitches: Straight stitch, couching, pattern stitch.

Technique: Stitches used in combination. Embroider before seaming sides, as a great deal of turning is necessary. Remember to keep needle down when turning.

Design Source: Museum of Natural History; Greek, African, American Indian designs.

FLOWERED BAGS

Stitches: Free-surface machine embroidery, couching.

Technique: Free-surface machine embroidery and couching used, with textured contrasts in bag fabrics (cotton, canvas, and burlap). If fabric is stiff, no backing is necessary; if not, use a hoop or backing.

Fabric: Cotton canvas is preferable. Be sure your fabric has body, whatever the choice.

Design Source: A tree design could be effective. Good sources are flowers, folk art, and nature.

HEALTH FOOD SHOPPING BAG
By Jeanette Feldman

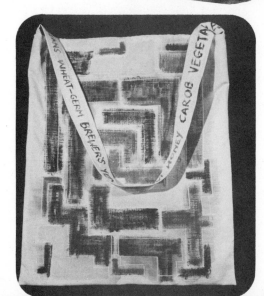

Stitches: Satin stitch.

Technique: Satin stitch used to accent lines, painted with thinned acrylic water-base paint.

Fabric: Heavy cotton, duck.

Variations: More pattern stitching can be used to advantage.

Design Source: Hard-edge paintings.

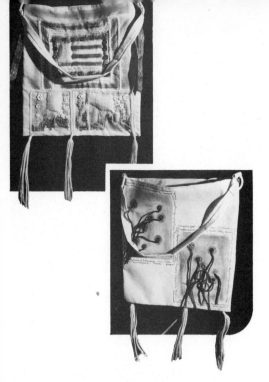

AMERICAN FLAG BAG
By Jeanette Feldman

Stitches: Appliqué, satin stitch, couching.

Technique: On front of bag, direct application of fabric bands; on back, rectangular shapes embroidered first, then appliquéd and secured by satin stitch. Handles and tassels on front and back formed by couching on yarn.

Fabric: Sturdy cotton canvas or similar synthetic.

Design Source: Consult library for flag design, Museum of Natural History for examples of banners with dripping or tasseled effects. Observe especially African, Peruvian, and American Indian designs.

CLOTHES FOR ALL OCCASIONS

SHIRTWAIST DRESS
Courtesy Simplicity Pattern Company

Stitches: Pattern stitch.

Technique: Pattern stitch makes a simple shirtwaist dress something special. The pattern requires more control when the foot is riding on seam allowances. Back fabric with typing paper.

Fabric: Cotton or synthetic.

Design Source: Stich Catalog; sewing machine manual.

TWO-PIECE DRESS
Courtesy Simplicity Pattern Company

Stitches: Pattern stitch, zigzag stitch.

Technique: Pattern stitch and zigzag in red, purple, and black on gray, on top and skirt front and sides.

Fabric: Velvet.

Design Source: Stitch Catalog. See your sewing machine manual for pattern stitch combinations.

PATTERNED BLOUSE
Courtesy Simplicity Pattern Company

Stitches: Zigzag stitch, double-needle stitch.

Technique: An exquisitely delicate pattern in brown and burnt orange edges the blouse; zigzag stitch, width 1¾ and length 1¾, is used with a double hemstitch needle. The necklace is placed not to touch the facing. Sleeves and hems are encircled just above the hems.

Design Source: Stitch Catalog.

NECKLINE TREATMENTS

Pattern-stitch Necklace

Stitches:	Pattern stitch.
Technique:	Pattern stitch used on whole neckline; back fabric if it is not very firm.
Fabric:	Wool, or any fabric.
Design Source:	Stitch Catalog; ancient Egyptian, Persian, and Indian necklaces. Many museums have excellent collections.

By Regina Bartley

Fringed Neckline

Courtesy Simplicity Pattern Company

Stitches:	Tailor tack fringing, pattern stitch.
Technique:	Tailor tacking used for all fringe, pattern stitch used to secure and decorate fringe. Fringe can also be secured with a single straight stitch.
Fabric:	Silk jersey.
Design Source:	Stitch Catalog.

Yemenite Blouse

Courtesy American-Israeli Cultural Center, New York

Stitches:	Pattern stitch, satin stitch, free-surface machine embroidery, zigzag.
Technique:	Pattern stitches used in any combination, solid lines of satin stitch. Free-surface machine embroidery can duplicate pattern effects, and zigzag fills in narrow bands.
Fabric:	Cotton, silk, velvet.
Design Source:	Near Eastern folk art.

PATTERN-STITCHED DESIGNS

Machine-Embroidered Blouse

By Michika Sato

Stitches:	Couching, zigzag stitch, satin stitch, pattern stitch.
Technique:	Couching and zigzag stitch used together to couch embroidery floss into loops; loops formed by pulling extra floss away from stitch area until desired size loop is obtained, then continuing to stitch from the same point as before. Satin stitch used for heavier lines; pattern stitch completes design. Varying thread colors adds interest.
Fabric:	Cotton, no-iron synthetics, velvet, silk, or anything appropriate.
Design Source:	American Indian designs, Stitch Catalog.

Indian Dress
By Michika Sato

      Stitches: Pattern stitch.

   Technique: Entire design worked with various pattern stitches.

       Fabric: Cotton (back fabric for best results); velvet, gauze.

Design Sources: Stitch Catalog.

PEASANT BLOUSE
Courtesy Simplicity Pattern Company

      Stitches: Pattern stitch, satin stitch, varied stitch width satin stitch.

   Technique: All of these stitches are used in this stylized geometric flower design. Remember to practice on the same fabric before embroidering.

       Fabric: Indian gauze cotton or anything with a similar peasant look; velvet.

Design Source: Folk art, especially Pennsylvania Dutch.

PATTERN-STITCH-TRIM BLOUSE

      Stitches: Pattern stitch.

   Technique: Pattern stitch used for all lines of embroidery. For single half-moons on collar, determine where the beginning of the pattern stitch is located and work from this point. If your machine does not have an indicator, practice on a scrap of cloth.

       Fabric: Cotton, wash and wear, synthetic.

Design Source: Stitch Catalog.

FLOWER GARLAND
Courtesy American-Israeli Cultural Center, New York

      Stitches: Free-surface machine embroidery, couching.

   Technique: The entire design is worked in a combination of free-surface embroidery and couching. The couched lines can be worked from the reverse or the right side. Use a hoop, and typing paper if you are working from the right side.

       Fabric: Cotton or other suitable fabric.

  Variations: Continue the graceful curve of the garland down the front, or around the entire dress. Full sleeves can be embroidered with garlands of couched flowers.

Design Source: Persian miniatures, illuminated manuscripts, old English type.

SPECIAL DRESSES
Embroidery by Regina Bartley; courtesy Simplicity Pattern Company

     Stitches: Pattern stitch, double-needle stitch.

   Technique: Pattern stitch combination used for trim on dress with crisp white collar and cuffs; a double needle pattern stitch, stitch width 3, stitch length 1½, is used for serpentine lines on long apron dress. To be sure patterns are straight, draw guidelines lightly on fabric before you begin. Back fabric with typing paper.

       Fabric: For trimmed dress, wool-like synthetic with cotton collar and cuffs; for apron dress, eyelet-embroidered cotton.

Design Source: Stitch Catalog.

QUILTED SKIRT
Courtesy American-Israeli Cultural Center, New York

     Stitches: Quilting, straight stitch, optional trapunto.

   Technique: The skirt is lined, with a thin layer of batting used between fabric and lining. The design on the fabric is the guide for quilting lines. Straight stitch is used with a stitch width of 1 for a whipped look to the stitched line, and selected areas of fabric pattern can be accented with trapunto.

       Fabric: Any appropriate material.

Design Source: Fabric collections.

PEACOCK DRESS
Courtesy Simplicity Pattern Company

     Stitches: Pattern stitch, satin stitch.

   Technique: Pattern stitch used for all pattern lines in tail; satin stitch used for all outlines and fine lines fanning out at bottom.

       Fabric: Cotton.

Design Source: Stitch Catalog.

YEMENITE BLOUSE
Courtesy American-Israeli Cultural Center, New York

     Stitches: Free-surface machine embroidery, couching.

   Technique: Design worked in couching from reverse side, with embroidery floss, fine yarn, or cord in the bobbin. As an alternative to working from the reverse, free-surface machine embroidery is also used, with embroidery floss threaded through hole in embroidery presser foot or placed front to back through the part of the presser foot where the

needle goes up and down. Hold floss lightly as you embroider, if necessary.

Fabric: Cotton, velvet, or any suitable material.

Design Source: Near Eastern folk art.

COUCHED RED AND GOLD SKIRT

Stitches: Couching, free-surface machine embroidery.

Technique: Couching can be worked with free-floating couching satin stitch technique. Free-surface machine embroidery is worked with embroidery floss in bobbin, spool thread the same color, stitch width 1.

Fabric: Black homespun cotton or other suitable material. Embroidery floss is very silky, rich gold and red.

Variations: Couched shapes can be scattered, in stripes, or circular.

Design Source: Folk art; sketches.

BLUE SKIRT
Courtesy Simplicity Pattern Company

Stitches: Pattern stitch, straight stitch.

Technique: Pattern stitch used for all except straight lines. Straight stitch used for straight lines between lines of pattern stitching bordering hem; embroidery floss in bobbin, spool thread matches skirt. Worked from reverse side. Use stitch width 1 for a whipped look.

Fabric: Wool or synthetic mix.

Design Source: Stitch Catalog.

ORIENTAL CAFTANS *(see color insert)*
Courtesy American-Israeli Cultural Center, New York

Stitches: Couching, straight stitch, zigzag stitch.

Technique: Couching used for entire design, worked from reverse side with straight stitch and on the right side with a narrow zigzag stitch. Thread can be the same color as the embroidery floss or cord, a contrasting color, or an invisible nylon.

Fabric: Cotton; satin; silk, synthetic, or velvet.

Design Source: Near Eastern arabesque and embroideries, iron grille work, illuminated manuscripts. Consult your library and museums.

FLORAL-EMBROIDERED DRESSES AND BLOUSES
Courtesy Simplicity Pattern Company

Stitches: Appliqué, satin stitch, pattern stitch, free-surface machine embroidery, couching.

Technique: Any one, a combination, or all of the stitches listed can be used to embroider these flower designs. These designs are available as iron-on patterns from Simplicity. This approach could also be used for a tablecloth or place mats.

Fabric: Any suitable material. If fabric is not firm, use a hoop or backing.

Design Source: Seed catalogs, flower paintings, folk art (Spanish, Mexican, Hungarian).

POCKET POWER

Stitches: Satin stitch, varied stitch width satin stitch, free-surface machine embroidery, straight stitch, couching..

Technique: Satin stitch and varied stitch width satin stitch used for all broad lines; free-surface machine embroidery used for the rest of the design. Thin lines worked in straight stitch. Couching, with embroidery floss in the bobbin and working from the reverse side, can be used on stem and leaves; heavy lines of satin stitching can also be padded by couching embroidery floss under them. Work from the right side with the embroidery floss through the hole in the presser foot or placed between the toes of the presser foot. For patch pockets, experiment with cut work on various fabrics. Embroider pocket before attaching it.

Fabric: Cotton or synthetic wash and wear; contrasting fabrics.

Design Source: Nature, nature books.

JACKETS AND SUITS

Smart originality can be added here with simple lapel designs, borders, and pocket designs, or with impressively rich embroidery on jacket backs and pants legs. Embroidered strips down the sides of skirts or pants legs can be stunning.

WHITE SUIT
Courtesy Simplicity Pattern Company

Stitches: Pattern stitch.

Technique: This handsomely patterned suit is a project for the more skilled, but it is really worth the practice it takes to match up the pattern lines. Use extra care when turning corners; remember to back fabric when stitching.

Fabric: Sharkskin, cotton, rayon, or any crisp, firm fabric.

Design Source: Stitch Catalog.

JEANS JACKETS

Birds by the Light of the Moon *and* **How Lovely Your Flowers Grow!**
By Linda Sampson

Stitches: Appliqué, satin stitch.

Technique: Appliqué figures, patterns and solids, are sewed on and excess fabric cut away carefully; satin stitch secures and accents shapes.

Fabric: Cotton.

Design Source: Fabric shops; photographs and prints.

Hurrah For The House On The Hill
By Linda Sampson

Stitches: Appliqué, satin stitch, varied stitch width satin stitch, couching.

Technique: Appliqué used for all shapes; satin stitch secures and outlines shapes, forms the rainbow, and trims color areas. Varied stitch width satin stitch forms outline of house, and rickrack rays of the sun are couched on.

Fabric: Cotton. Satin and velvet can also be used.

Design Source: Children's books; greeting cards.

SLEEVELESS JACKET
Courtesy Simplicity Pattern Company

Stitches: Pattern stitch.

Technique: Fine lines of accented pattern stitch give jacket a rich but subtle look; the same lines that trim the yoke can be used down the sides of matching pants. Experiment with various stitch lengths and widths; be sure to match patterns.

Fabric: Cotton corduroy.

Design Source: Stitch Catalog.

COATS AND CAPES

APPLIQUÉ COAT

By Lillian Delevoryas, Weatherall Workshops, Coleford, Gloucestershire, England

Stitches: Appliqué, satin stitch, pattern stitch, free-surface machine embroidery.

Technique: All shapes are appliquéd, secured and accented with satin stitch. Satin stitch also used to heighten forms by drawing within shapes. Pattern stitch used decoratively within appliquéd shapes; free-surface machine embroidery used to work brocade of flowers on the sleeves.

Fabric: Velvets, silks, and satins juxtaposed with elegant woven patterns of upholstery materials. Fabric textures and colors play an important role in creating the beauty of this coat.

Design Source: Folk art, travel posters, textile designs, wallpaper; the paintings of Henri Rousseau; nature.

SEWN PAINTINGS AS DECORATION
Fairway Frolic at Firefly, *detail*
By Joan Blumenbaum

  Stitches: Free-surface machine embroidery, appliqué, satin stitch, trapunto, pattern stitch.

  Technique: Background figures are appliqué, secured and accented by satin stitch and pattern stitches. Figure is developed with free-surface machine embroidery on silkscreen; trapunto accents background areas. Work the figure before seaming the coat.

  Fabric: Wool, cotton, or any firm material. Be sure to back fabric.

Design Source: Photographs.

PATTERN-STITCHED CAPE
Courtesy Simplicity Pattern Company

  Stitches: Double needle, pattern stitch, satin stitch.

  Technique: Pattern stitch worked with double and single needles; solid lines are satin stitched. Embroider ties before attaching to cape. Work on two thicknesses of material; back with tape if fabric is not available.

  Fabric: Lightweight wool or synthetic combination.

Design Source: Stitch Catalog.

APPLIQUÉD CAPE
Courtesy 1,001 Sewing and Needlecraft Ideas

  Stitches: Pattern stitches, free-surface machine embroidery, appliqué.

  Technique: Pattern stitch edges collar and sleeves and the circle design on the front; free-surface machine embroidery is used for the motif in the center. The circle design can be appliquéd directly on the cape or stitched down after it has been embroidered on another piece of fabric or applied with an iron-on product. The center motif can be a small appliqué.

  Fabric: Firm fabric with a hard or soft finish.

Variations: The circle design can be several smaller circles of just pattern stitches. Circles can be placed on the cape around the hem or down one sleeve or as a repeat design down the front. Experiment with cut-out circles on a drawing or photograph of a cape.

Design Source: Stitch Catalog.

SPORTSWEAR

ICE SKATING SKIRT
Courtesy Michael Futterman, New York

Stitches: Pattern stitch, couching, free-surface machine embroidery, varied stitch width satin stitch, straight stitch.

Technique: Pattern stitch used for dots in top linear leaf, zigzagged line below flowers, all flowers and two center leaves, center stem. Flowers couched with embroidery floss. Free-surface machine embroidery can be used for the zigzagged line and the straight lines. Embroidery floss should be wound in the bobbin and the design worked from the reverse side. Varied stitch width satin stitch forms curved line from stem of top leaf; straight stitch used in forward-reverse technique for top leaf. Can also be used for straight lines, with embroidery floss on the bobbin and design worked from reverse side. For heavier straight lines, set the machine at stitch width 1 to give a whipped look to the thread.

Fabric: Any suitable material.

Design Source: Flower prints, Stitch Catalog.

SWIMSUIT OR BIKINI *(see color insert)*
By Anne Barnaby

Stitches: Appliqué, satin stitch, pattern stitch.

Technique: Appliqué used for large design areas, satin stitch used for linear effects. Pattern stitch embellishes pattern edges and accents stripes.

Fabric: Soft cotton or synthetic; experiment with stretch fabrics. Back with an iron-on product. Cut out the bikini's lining when you cut the fabric.

Variations: Satin stitch a textile design to a solid background, cut away close to stitching, and intertwine the appliquéd shapes with pattern stitches.

Design Source: Books on tropical flowers, fish, etc.; textile or fabric designs, abstract designs in wrought iron; folk or modern art.

UNDERCLOTHES

BIKINI PANTIES

Stitches:	Pattern stitch.
Technique:	Ready-made panties trimmed (top) and edged (bottom) with pattern stitches. Back with typing paper.
Fabric:	Nylon.
Design Source:	Stitch Catalog.

SLIP

Courtesy Michael Futterman, New York

Stitches:	Couching, satin stitch, pattern stitch.
Technique:	All lines couched with embroidery floss in the bobbin, using satin stitch, from reverse side. Pattern stitch used for scalloped line.
Fabric:	Nylon or any appropriate material.
Design Source:	Other lingerie, fashion books, fashion history books.

APPLIQUÉD LACE ON SLIP

Stitches:	Free-surface machine embroidery, satin stitch, appliqué, cut work.
Technique:	Free-surface machine embroidery and satin stitch used together to form flowers, stems, and leaves directly on slip; hemline scalloped with satin stitch. Lace appliqué is attached to the slip with a fine satin stitch and excess cut away. Fabric behind the lace is carefully cut away.
Fabric:	Nylon.
Design Source:	Other lingerie.

FORMAL WEAR

VELVET EVENING BAG

Stitches:	Free-surface machine embroidery.
Technique:	All lines worked from reverse with gold Lurex in bobbin. Use hoop to keep fabric taut; seam sides of bag after embroidering.
Fabric:	Red velvet.
Design Source:	Stitch Catalog.

By Regina Bartley

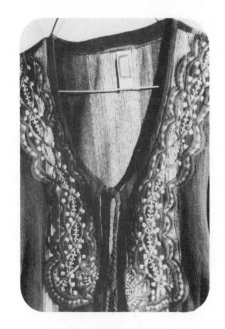

ORIENTAL ROBE
Courtesy American-Israeli Cultural Center, New York

Stitches: Satin stitch, varied stitch width satin stitch, pattern stitch.

Technique: Satin stitch used for all wide lines, greater interest is achieved with threads of various colors. Varied stitch width satin stitch outlines flower petals. Dots can be made this way or with pattern stitch, used for spiked lines.

Fabric: Heavy homespun cotton; velvet.

Design Source: Near Eastern folk art; Stitch Catalog.

CAFTAN

Stitches: Pattern stitch, zigzag stitch, satin stitch.

Technique: Pattern stitch follows all seams and hemline in parallel lines; zigzag or satin stitch can also be used.

Sewing Instructions: The pattern requires 4⅔ yards of 54-inch material, or seam strip to a narrower width if desired. A strip can be added on either side; try a contrasting color or pattern. The fabric base is 84 by 54 inches.

Fold fabric in half and lay it flat; fold in half again to a 42-by-54-inch piece. Cut a curve on the 54-inch side, starting 24 inches from the top and stopping 16 inches from the bottom. The 42-inch side should now measure 26 inches.

Unfold once, into two large half-ovals. Seam; cut apart along remaining fold after seaming. The seam must be open in three places to allow for the hands and head—six inches for hands, ten inches for head.

Stitch along the 84-inch line: stitch 14 inches, skip six inches; stitch 17 inches, skip ten inches; stitch seven inches, skip six inches; stitch 14 inches. Try caftan; shorten if necessary. If possible, shorten before cutting curves.

Fabric: No-iron chiffon synthetic; soft velvet; any soft easy-care fabric.

Design Source: Indian saris, folk costumes.

EVENING WRAP *(see color insert)*

Stitches: Pattern stitch.

Technique: Cuffs, collar, hem, or all are encircled with pattern stitching. Pattern stitching can also be started at

the neckline in two bold diagonals to form an inverted V down to the hem; to keep the fabric from puckering, place a length of tape under the area to be stitched. Back with typing paper.

Fabric: Velvet. Be sure to back if fabric is not doubled or very firm.

Design Source: Stitch Catalog.

ITALIAN QUILTED EVENING JACKET
Courtesy Michael Futterman, New York

Stitches: Italian quilting.

Technique: A simple design is repeated over entire jacket, subtly varied with rich Italian quilting relief.

Fabric: Satin. Other rich fabrics, such as Quiana, would be beautiful and easier to maintain.

Design Source: Nature; books.

EVENING CAPE
Courtesy Michael Futterman, New York

Stitches: Appliqué, couching.

Technique: Cut a shape you like and appliqué to cape neckline; couch gold cord to form a diamond-shaped grid, or a more fluid design.

Fabric: Rich brocades, silk, satin.

Design Source: Fashion history books.

LOUNGE AND SLEEPWEAR

AT-HOME DRESS

Stitches: Appliqué, satin stitch, free-surface machine embroidery, couching, straight stitch.

Technique: Cornucopia is appliquéd in same fabric as dress; satin stitch secures and decorates with a wide stitch width around the mouth and a narrow one around the sides. Free-surface machine embroidery used for berries; larger fruit, stems, and leaves worked with satin stitch, free-surface embroidery, and couching, from reverse side; embroidery floss in the bobbin. Stitch width 1 used for a whipped look.

Fabric: Cotton; wash and wear synthetic.

Design Source: Early American folk art, Pennsylvania Dutch art; greeting cards.

RUFFLED NIGHTGOWN

Stitches: Satin stitch.

Technique: Hem edged with three lines of satin stitch in various colors; ruffles edged with single line.

Fabric: Cotton.

Design Source: Stitch Catalog.

DRAGON LADY SILK KIMONO

Stitches: Satin stitch, varied stitch width satin stitch, free-surface machine embroidery.

Technique: Satin stitch used for all even width lines, varied stitch width satin stitch for others. Free-surface machine embroidery used to work solid areas; white lines on dragon's back are satin stitched on after free-surface work.

Fabric: Silk.

Design Source: Chinese and Japanese art.

LOUNGING PAJAMAS

Courtesy Michael Futterman, New York

Stitches: Couching, free-surface machine embroidery, varied stitch width satin stitch, pattern stitch.

Technique: All larger areas couched with embroidery floss; free-surface machine embroidery can be used instead. Varied stitch width satin stitch used for all smaller areas. Pattern stitch can be substituted where appropriate. Back fabric before stitching.

Fabric: Silk; soft synthetic; fine cotton. Choose no-iron material, if possible.

Design Source: Chinese and Japanese art; nature.

NIGHTGOWN NECKLINE IDEAS

Stitches: Satin stitch, pattern stitch.

Technique: Scalloped edges are stitched with satin stitch or pattern stitch; excess fabric is then cut away. Varicolored thread is used. Pattern stitch forms flowers. Back with typing paper and stretch in hoop.

Fabric: Cotton; nylon or other appropriate synthetic.

Design Source: Greeting cards; Persian miniatures.

SMOCKED GOWN AND NEGLIGÉE

Stitches: Pattern stitch, satin stitch, gathering with zigzag stitch.

Technique: Satin stitch edges neckline. Ruffled effect is produced by zigzag stitching on unbacked fabric; pull fabric while stitching. More pulling gives greater ruffling. Pattern stitch is used over or beside zigzag. Sleeve edges can be treated in the same manner as the yoke.

Fabric: Soft cotton or synthetic.

Design Source: Ready-made sleepwear; fashion history books.

ROBES

Robe with Embroidered Trim

Stitches: Pattern stitch.

Technique: Pattern stitch worked on separate strip of organdy, then attached with lace. Use a small loop for each flower, or work rows of pattern stitches, varicolored rows of satin stitches, or varied stitch width satin stitch.

Fabric: Organdy; velvet.

Design Source: Stitch Catalog.

Casual Robe
Courtesy Simplicity Pattern Company

Stitches: Pattern stitch.

Technique: Pattern stitch used as edging around collar, cuffs, and belt. If fabric is not too soft, no backing is needed.

Fabric: Wool or a napped synthetic.

Design Source: Stitch Catalog; other pattern-stitched clothing in this book.

Robe with Embroidered Panel

Stitches: Pattern stitch, varied stitch width satin stitch, satin stitch.

Technique: All stitches used as the appearance of the stitched panel indicates. The panel can be embroidered and stitched to the robe afterwards; the fabric of the panel need not be the same as that of the robe.

Fabric: Soft flannel; silk, velvet; synthetic.

Design Source: Oriental rugs; scrollwork in illuminated manuscripts; Stitch Catalog.

embroidery for men

TIES

Embroidery patterns for these accessories should be simple and uncomplicated. Stripes are easy to do and can produce a handsome effect.

TIE IDEAS

Stitches: Pattern stitch, free-surface machine embroidery, zigzag stitch.

Technique: Pattern stitch forms stripes and borders; no backing is necessary. Free-surface machine embroidery with zigzag used to work dogs and polo player. The motif could be a golfer, a swimmer, or any other sportsman; an antique key or a fleur-de-lis could also be handsome. A double needle makes striking diagonal pattern lines.

Fabric: Dogs on corduroy, polo player on fine wool; vertical pattern lines on silk, horizontal lines on cotton.

Design Source: Stitch Catalog.

BELTS

Casual men's slacks are more attractive when worn with a jaunty embroidered belt, buckled or made to tie with fringed ends. A large wood or brass buckle can be very effective. Stitch the belt fabric around buckram for a stiff belt, or rehabilitate an old belt.

FLOWER-TRIMMED BELT

Stitches: Free-surface machine embroidery, pattern stitch, appliqué.

Technique: Flowers are worked with free-surface machine embroidery on a separate piece of fabric; pattern stitch can also be used for the design. The panel is appliquéd or attached with an iron-on product.

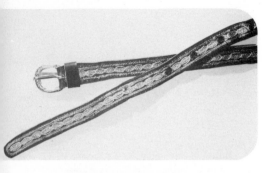

Fabric: Leather or cloth. A whole belt can be embroidered directly if it is soft enough for your machine.

Design Source: Borders on garments and art.

COUCHED BELT

Stitches: Straight stitch, couching, zigzag stitch.

Technique: Couching with straight stitch, stitch width 1, used from the reverse side, with embroidery floss in the bobbin. Or zigzag stitch, stitch width 2 or 2½, can be used from the right side, with the embroidery floss through the hole in the embroidery presser foot or between the presser toes.

Fabric: Leather; any firm material. Use a special needle if your machine requires it.

Design Source: Stitch Catalog.

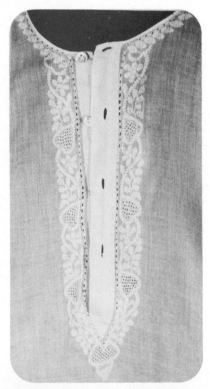

SHIRTS

HEMSTITCHED SHIRT

Stitches: Hemstitch and trellis work, pattern stitch, satin stitch, couching.

Technique: Hemstitch encirles the neckline and placket; trellis work used to work large leaf forms. Small leaves and flowers worked with pattern stitch, and undulating stem lines with satin stitch. Pattern stitch and satin stitch are then clipped carefully, as described in the Stitch Catalog section on couching, to create a soft napped look.

Fabric: Soft cotton or Indian cotton gauze.

Design Source: Book endpapers, Near Eastern art.

PEASANT SHIRT
Courtesy Simplicity Pattern Company

Stitches: Pattern stitch, satin stitch, varied stitch width satin stitch.

Technique: All stitches are used in a stylized geometric flower design. Practice on the same or a similar fabric before embroidering.

Fabric: Light cotton; any light, rough-weave material; velvet.

Design Source: Folk art, expecially Pennsylvania Dutch and Mexican.

BLUE-ON-BLUE DRESS SHIRT

Stitches: Hemstitch, pattern stitch, varied stitch width satin stitch.

Technique: Undulating vertical lines worked with single-needle hemstitch, rest of design with pattern stitch. Varied stitch width satin stitch can be used with or instead of pattern stitch. For a less ambitious approach, embroider only the front placket and the hemstitched lines on either side. Vertical lines of pattern stitch are much easier to work. Back fabric.

Fabric: Any suitable shirting.

Design Source: Stitch Catalog.

SPANISH ELEGANCE

Stitches: Circular pattern stitch, free-surface machine embroidery.

Technique: Circular pattern stitching used for small figures and for outside of large figures; free-surface machine embroidery used to work center texture of large figures. Draw design carefully and practice first. Some machines have a special attachment for circular embroidery. Be sure to back fabric.

Fabric: Any good shirt material.

Design Source: Spanish grille work; experiment with a compass.

COWBOY SHIRT, Prairie Flower

Stitches: Pattern stitch, varied stitch width satin stitch.

Technique: Dots formed with bead pattern on machine; remainder of design worked with varied stitch width satin stitch.

Fabric: A strong cotton.

Design Source: Western boots, saddles, folk art, flowers.

VESTS

VELVET VEST, Love Stars Vibrations

Stitches: Varied stitch width satin stitch, pattern stitch, satin stitch.

Technique: Varied stitch width satin stitch forms undulating lines above and below circles; pattern stitch done freely around stars forms circles. Stars are satin stitched points, circle, and cross. Stars worked first, next the circles, and undulating lines last.

By Regina Bartley

Design can also go around the neckline, border the bottom, accent the pockets, or encircle the buttonholes.

Fabric: Dark blue velvet.

Design Source: Pictures of flowers, magnified details in nature. Stitch Catalog.

DETAILING FOR VEST OR SWEATER

Stitches: Free-surface machine embroidery.

Technique: Free-surface embroidery used with zigzag for entire design. Do not use hoop; use iron-on product and typing paper. Knits stretch easily.

Fabric: Knits; any suitable fabric.

Design Source: Sporting goods stores, sports magazines.

JACKETS

COUCHED DRAGON DETAIL
Courtesy Michael Futterman, New York

Stitches: Couching, free-surface machine embroidery, straight stitch.

Technique: Straight stitch and free-surface embroidery used together, worked from reverse with embroidery floss in the bobbin. Use hoop for best results.

Fabric: Sturdy cotton or synthetic.

Design Source: Oriental art; nature; any suitable motif.

JACKET LANDSCAPE
Jacket and photo by Linda Sampson

Stitches: Appliqué, satin stitch, pattern stitch.

Technique: All shapes appliquéd. Satin stitch secures and accents shapes and forms curving road in middle section. Pattern stitch used for borders, middle section.

Fabric: Silk, cotton, upholstery fabrics on cotton or velvet.

Design Source: Landscapes; impressionist paintings.

SPORT JACKET
Courtesy Simplicity Pattern Company

Stitches: Pattern stitch, zigzag stitch.

Technique: Pattern stitch decorates placket inside and out; black lines worked in zigzag, stitch width 4, stitch length 3/4—almost a satin stitch. No backing necessary. Pattern can also decorate cuffs, collar, or pockets, or down pants seams.

Fabric: Firm cotton or wash and wear synthetic.

Design Source: Stitch Catalog.

COCKATOO JACKET
By Rick Rogers; courtesy Levi-Strauss & Co.

Stitches: Free-surface machine embroidery, zigzag stitch, varied stitch width satin stitch.

Technique: Free-surface machine embroidery with zigzag stitch can be used to work entire design. Garland lines around bird, lines of flowers, stem, and open flowers are varied stitch width satin stitch. Parts of the design may adapt to pattern stitches on your machine. Back fabric.

Fabric: Denim.

Design Source: Any suitable motif.

JACKET SUNSET
By Nancy Merkel; courtesy Levi-Strauss & Co.

Stitches: Free-surface machine embroidery, zigzag stitch, satin stitch, couching.

Technique: Free-surface embroidery with zigzag used to work sky and road. Couching forms textured tree, with looped and stitched method shown with heavy yarn in Stitch Catalog. Satin stitch outlines mountains.

Fabric: Denim.

Design Source: Sierra Club nature books.

DRESSING GOWNS AND SMOKING JACKETS

COUCHED DRESSING GOWN
Courtesy Michael Futterman, New York

Stitches: Couching, pattern stitch.

Technique: Couch a simple arabesque of twisted narrow ribbon to trim collar and lapels. Use an open pattern stitch.

Fabric: Any suitable material.

Design Source: Art nouveau; illuminated manuscripts.

SMOKING JACKET
Courtesy Michael Futterman, New York

Stitches: Couching.

Technique: Entire design is worked with simple couching of embroidery floss. The lapels can also be bordered with several rows of pattern stitches.

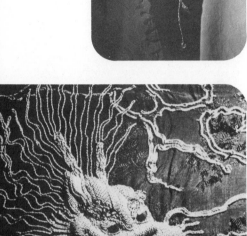

Fabric: Velvet collar on brocaded silk.

Design Source: Fashion history books; Renaissance costume.

ORIENTAL DRESSING GOWN DESIGN
Courtesy Michael Futterman, New York

Stitches: Couching, trapunto.

Technique: Entire design is gold thread simply couched on a rich black brocade. Dragons are stuffed with yarn, couched first in the other direction. Threads are separated to show padding.

Fabric: Silk, satin, brocade.

Design Source: Oriental art.

VELOUR DRESSING GOWN

Stitches: Pattern stitch.

Technique: Contrasting bands of velour trim front panels and cuffs; pattern stitching secures and accents bands.

Fabric: Velour.

Design Source: Stitch Catalog.

clothes and accessories for kids

SMOCKS, APRONS, AND PINAFORES

Simple designs can do a lot to liven up children's clothes. Appliqué, pattern-stitched stripes, and smocking can all make forgettable clothes something special.

APPLIQUÉD ROMPERS AND PINAFORES *(see color insert)*

Stitches: Appliqué, satin stitch, straight stitch.

Technique: Appliqué forms all shapes; satin stitch secures and accents. Straight stitch secures forms.

Fabric: Cotton or synthetic wash and wear.

Design Source: Nursery books, greeting cards.

EMBROIDERED APPLIQUÉ *(see color insert)*

Stitches: Appliqué, satin stitch, zigzag stitch, couching, free-surface machine embroidery.

Technique: Appliqué forms all large shapes; satin or zigzag stitch secures and accents. Couching used for stems and leaves, hair, and butterflies. Free-surface machine embroidery used for further designs on appliquéd forms. Butterfly shapes can be attached only in the center by couching. The wings can then flap freely. If you do this, be sure to finish wing edges with a close zigzag or satin stitch.

Fabric: No-iron wash and wear cotton or synthetic.

Design Source: Nursery rhyme books, children's books.

ANIMAL BIBS
Courtesy The Gazebo, New York

Stitches: Quilting, appliqué, satin stitch, couching.

Technique: Bib is quilted, with animal shapes appliquéd on; satin stitch secures and accents. Accents of grass and flowers are couched. Animals can be appliquéd before or after fabric is quilted.

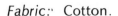
Fabric: Cotton.

Design Source: Nursery books.

SMOCKED PINAFORE

Stitches: Smocking stitch, satin or pattern stitch.

Technique: Front panel of pinafore is smocked; use any of the smocking techniques. Satin stitch or pattern stitch can be embroidered over stitch lines of smocking in the same or in contrasting colors.

Fabric: Velveteen or any soft fabric.

Design Source: Stitch Catalog; fashion history books.

PANTS

SHORTS FOR ALL AGES

Stitches: Pattern stitch, free-surface machine embroidery, circular embroidery (top shorts); appliqué, satin stitch (bottom shorts).

Technique: Pattern stitch or free-surface machine embroidery is used for flowers; circular embroidery attachment simplifies the process. Back fabric or use hoop if fabric is not firm. Elephant, button shapes, and border on bibbed shorts are appliquéd; satin stitch secures shapes.

Fabric: Cotton, wash and wear, synthetic.

Design Source: Children's books.

APPLIQUÉD KITE SLACKS

Stitches: Satin stitch, appliqué, zigzag stitch, couching.

Technique: All shapes are appliquéd, then extra fabric is cut away. Satin stitch edges kite and tail and secures flowers on circle. Zigzag stitch holds center of kite, tail, and circle to pants legs. Couching can be used instead of zigzag.

Fabric: Cotton.

Design Source: Children's books.

VEST AND SHORTS

Stitches: Pattern stitch.

Technique: A simple pattern-stitched border is sewn around shorts and vest. No backing necessary.

Fabric: Dark green velvet.

Design Source: Stitch Catalog.

By Regina Bartley

SHIRTS, AND DRESSES

SUPERHERO SHIRT

Stitches: Appliqué, satin stitch.

Technique: All shapes are appliqué, secured and accented with satin stitch. Back fabric to avoid puckering; do not use hoop.

Fabric: Velvet and terrycloth.

Design Source: Comic books.

By Regina Bartley

WESTERN SHIRTS

Stitches: Pattern stitch.

Technique: Pattern stitch follows seams and trims collars, cuffs, yoke, and placket.

Fabric: Wash and wear cotton.

Design Source: Stitch Catalog.

By Regina Bartley

APPLIQUÉ T-SHIRTS

Stitches: Appliqué, satin stitch, free-surface machine embroidery.

Technique: Larger shapes are appliquéd, secured and accented with satin stitch. Details and drawing worked with narrow satin stitch, free-surface embroidery.

Fabric: Cotton jersey.

Design Source: Children's books, comic books.

FANCY FLOWERS DRESS

Courtesy Simplicity Pattern Company

Stitches: Free-surface machine embroidery, pattern stitch, satin stitch, straight stitch.

Technique: Entire design can be worked with free-surface machine embroidery; pattern stitch used for dots and satin stitch for stems. Straight stitch, stitch width 1, can also be used for stems; use embroidery floss in the bobbin case and work from reverse side. Embroidery pattern available from Simplicity.

Fabric: Any light material; velvet.

Design Source: Seed catalogs, Pennsylvania Dutch design, books on flowers.

SQUARE-YOKED DRESS

       Stitches: Couching.

    Technique: Entire design is couched with fine yarn; patterned fabric is used for background.

        Fabric: Cotton or any no-iron or wash and wear fabric.

Design Source: Fabric swatches and catalogs.

THE BIG APPLE DRESS

       Stitches: Free-surface machine embroidery, appliqué, pattern stitch.

    Technique: Free-surface machine embroidery forms apples and leaves on a solid background; fabric strip appliquéd to dress. Pattern stitch borders appliqué strip. Braid can also be used as edging.

        Fabric: Cotton, wash and wear, or synthetic.

Design Source: Children's books, seed catalogs.

SWEATER DESIGNS

COUCHED DETAILS

       Stitches: Couching, free-surface machine embroidery.

    Technique: Solid areas are couched with textured yarn like bouclé. Lines can be couched or worked with free-surface embroidery, straight stitch, stitch width 1, from the reverse side, with yarn in the bobbin case.

        Fabric: Any suitable knit.

Design Source: Children's books, greeting cards, your child's drawings.

SWEATER EMBROIDERY

       Stitches: Free-surface machine embroidery.

    Technique: Entire design worked with free-surface embroidery. Back with an iron-on product and typing paper; do not use a hoop.

        Fabric: Knit.

Design Source: Children's books, greeting cards, posters, record albums.

COATS AND JACKETS

FREE-SURFACE JACKET EMBROIDERY *(see color insert)*

       Stitches: Free-surface machine embroidery.

    Technique: Any design can be worked with free-surface embroidery. The jacket fabric is firm enough not to need a hoop; hold down well to the machine with your fingertips, moving it gently.

Fabric: Soft leather or leatherlike vinyl.

Design Source: Any simple motif that is mostly lines; children's books; any drawing.

Siesta JEANS JACKET

Stitches: Free-surface machine embroidery, zigzag stitch, varied stitch width satin stitch, satin stitch, couching.

Technique: Entire design worked with zigzag stitch in free-surface machine embroidery; or varied stitch width satin stitch and satin stitch can be used for lines; rays of the sun can be couched from reverse side or the right side of jacket, with embroidery floss.

Fabric: Denim.

Design Source: Travel posters, comic books, children's books.

FUR-TRIMMED COAT WITH COUCHED ARABESQUE

Stitches: Appliqué, couching, zigzag stitch.

Technique: Appliqué used for flower shapes; arabesque lines couched with zigzag stitch. Machine thread should be darker for contrast. Couched line can be yarn, embroidery floss, a fine strip of leather, or anything suitable.

Fabric: Any coat material.

Design Source: Persian miniatures, Oriental rugs, Swiss folk art.

ALPINE FLOWERS COAT

Stitches: Couching.

Technique: Couching worked from reverse side, with embroidery floss in the bobbin, stitch width 1, or on the surface with floss threaded through the hole in the embroidery presser foot or placed between the toes. Spool thread is the same color as floss. Whole yoke of coat can be so decorated, cuffs and hem trimmed.

Fabric: Sturdy winter-weight wool.

Design Source: Swiss folk art, illuminated manuscripts, greeting cards.

ACCESSORIES

BLUEBIRD BAG FOR LUNCH, BOOKS, OR BEACH
By Stephanie Natta

Stitches:	Appliqué, satin stitch.
Technique:	All shapes appliquéd, secured and outlined with satin stitch. Tiny butterflies and flower can be cut out of patterned chintz or flowered lace and appliquéd, with excess fabric then cut away.
Fabric:	Denim, satin, felt, or any suitable fabric.
Design Source:	Children's books, greeting cards, magazines.

TASSELED SCARF

Stitches:	Pattern stitch.
Technique:	Simple rows of white pattern stitch accent stripes on red and black muffler. Pattern stitch rows can also run vertically between stripes, or can create undulating free forms between them. Back with typing paper.
Fabric:	Knit.
Design Source:	Stitch Catalog.

HAT AND SCARF SET

Stitches:	Couching, free-surface machine embroidery.
Technique:	Free-floating couching used for entire design.
Fabric:	Knit.
Design Source:	Stitch Catalog.

HELMET HAT

Stitches:	Pattern stitch.
Technique:	Pattern stitching encircles face opening and neckline. Backing is optional; you may like the rippled effect of knit stitched without backing.
Fabric:	Knit.
Design Source:	Stitch Catalog.

HAT WITH A FLAIR

Stitches:	Satin stitch.
Technique:	Satin stitch edges brim of hat; fabric is stretched as it is embroidered to increase the rippled effect. Pattern stitching can be added in rows or in stripes.
Fabric:	Knit.
Design Source:	Stitch Catalog.

denims and beyond

JAZZY JEANS

SHORTS, Mushroom and Flowers
By Linda Sampson; photo, Vince Aiosa

     Stitches: Appliqué, satin stitch.

    Technique: All shapes are appliquéd, secured and outlined with satin stitch. No backing necessary.

      Fabric: Denim. Flowers are printed damask; background for mushrooms is velvet; mushrooms are gingham and cotton.

Design Source: Fabric swatches and catalogs; needlework patterns.

SHORTS, Birds, Flowers, and Butterfly *(see color insert)*
By Linda Sampson; photo, Vince Aiosa

     Stitches: Appliqué, satin stitch, straight stitch.

    Technique: All shapes are appliquéd, secured and enhanced with satin stitch. Gold Lurex in bobbin is straight stitched, worked from reverse side.

      Fabric: Denim with printed damask.

Design Source: Fabric swatches and catalogs; needlework patterns; greeting cards.

Fantasy from India EMBROIDERED APPLIQUÉ *(see color insert)*

     Stitches: Appliqué, satin stitch, couching, free-surface machine embroidery, pattern stitch, eyelet embroidery.

    Technique: Large solid areas are appliquéd, secured and accented with satin stitch. All heavy lines are couched with yarn or embroidery floss. Smaller solid areas and fine-line arabesques are worked with free-surface embroidery from reverse side, with fine yarn or embroidery floss in the bobbin. Use a straight stitch or stitch width 1. Bottom band worked with eyelet embroidery.

Fabric: Denim; velvet.

Design Source: Persian miniatures.

Hitchhiker POCKET PAINTING
By Ann Meske; courtesy Levi-Strauss & Co.

Stitches: Free-surface machine embroidery or couching.

Technique: Entire pocket is worked with either free-surface embroidery or couching. Use embroidery floss in the bobbin and work on reverse side, or couch embroidery floss on the right side.

Fabric: Denim.

Design Source: Landscapes, simplified and drawn on fabric.

FANCY PANTS
Jeans by Helen Bitar; courtesy Levi-Strauss & Co.

Stitches: Appliqué, satin stitch, couching, pattern stitch.

Technique: All shapes are appliquéd, secured and accented with satin stitch. Satin stitch used for all dots and almost all lines. Pockets, hips, and circular design on inside of pants legs worked with free-floating couching of embroidery floss; pattern stitch edges layered fabric on outside of the pants legs. Hoop or backing not necessary.

Fabric: Denim. Outside flaps are burlap, wool, cotton, and suede.

Design Source: Surrealistic art; album covers; any design that appeals.

SHIRTS AND BLOUSES

HUNGARIAN BLOUSES

Stitches: Free-surface machine embroidery, pattern stitch, smocking, couching, zigzag stitch.

Technique: Free-surface machine embroidery or pattern stitch can be used to work flower patterns; pattern stitch edges necklines, hemlines, and sleeves. Necklines, waistlines, and sleeves at wrists are smocked, with strands of embroidery floss couched over lines of smocking; or work from reverse side over smocking lines with a long, wide zigzag stitch, embroidery floss in the bobbin. Use hoop and backing.

Fabric: Cotton or any suitable material.

Design Source: Folk art and costumes.

APPLIQUÉD JERSEYS
Courtesy Simplicity Pattern Company

Stitches: Appliqué, satin stitch, varied stitch width satin stitch, pattern stitch.

Technique: Appliqué used for all shapes; satin stitch accents, secures, and draws faces. Varied stitch width satin stitch or pattern stitch can be used for lines of dots. Embroidery pattern available from Simplicity.

Fabric: Satin and velvet on cotton jersey.

Design Source: Magazines, posters, comic books.

FAN TANK TOP
Courtesy Simplicity Pattern Company

Stitches: Appliqué, pattern stitch, satin stitch.

Technique: Fan is embroidered separately and appliquéd to tank top; pattern stitch used for all pattern lines. Satin stitch secures appliqué and forms straight lines.

Fabric: Firm cotton on soft cotton knit.

Design Source: Any object.

JACKETS AND SWEATERS

LEVI JACKET
Courtesy Levi-Strauss & Co.

Stitches: Appliqué, satin stitch, free-surface machine embroidery.

Technique: All shapes are appliquéd, secured and outlined with bold satin stitch. Words worked with free-surface embroidery.

Fabric: Denim.

Design Source: Music albums, comic books.

JEANS JACKET WITH DOVE
By David Slopack; courtesy Levi-Strauss & Co.

Stitches: Appliqué, satin stitch, couching.

Technique: All shapes are appliquéd, secured with satin stitch. Satin stitch used to embroider face on sun in upper left corner, and can also be used for lines at bottom. Cloud lines couched with embroidery floss; can also be couched from reverse with floss in the bobbin, stitch width 1, thread same color as floss. Backing not necessary.

Fabric: Denim with cotton.

Design Source: Modern art; Oriental drawings and paintings of birds.

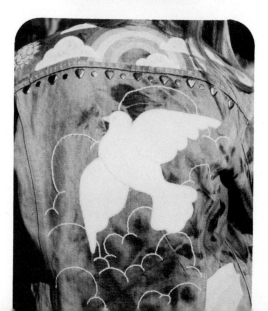

SUNDAE BEST
By Wendy Stitt; courtesy Levi-Strauss & Co.

Stitches:	Appliqué, satin stitch.
Technique:	All shapes are appliqué, secured with satin stitch. Notice strips of velvet bordered with buttons on sides of appliqué.
Fabric:	Satin on denim.
Design Source:	Ice cream parlor signs and menus.

THE OWL AND THE PUSSYCAT

Stitches:	Free-surface machine embroidery, appliqué, satin stitch, pattern stitch, varied stitch width satin stitch.
Technique:	Owl, cat, and duck worked in free-surface embroidery or appliqué secured with satin stitch. Pattern stitch or varied stitch width satin stitch used for line of flowers at shoulders. Backing or hoop may not be necessary; experiment.
Fabric:	Denim.
Design Source:	Children's books, nursery rhymes.

WORKER BLUES
By Kay Aronson; courtesy Levi-Strauss & Co.

Stitches:	Appliqué, satin stitch, trapunto.
Technique:	Faces are appliquéd directly to the jacket; satin stitch secures shapes and draws lines of the faces. Trapunto is used to pad faces; buttons are used decoratively on sleeves and shoulder line.
Fabric:	Denim.
Design Source:	Faces of any type or mood; nursery characters, superheroes, or rock stars; photographs.

COUCHED SWEATER

Stitches:	Couching, satin stitch.
Technique:	Small flowers and leaves worked with free-floating couching; larger flowers satin-stitched. Must be backed.
Fabric:	Knit.
Design Source:	Crewel work, early American embroidery designs; illuminated manuscripts; Swiss folk art.

UNIQUE ACCESSORIES

APPLIQUÉ FLOWER BAG
By Anne Barnaby

     Stitches: Appliqué, satin stitch.

     Technique: All shapes appliquéd, secured and outlined with satin stitch.

     Fabric: Cotton, felt, or any suitable material.

Design Source: Nature photography, seed catalogs.

A SKIRT WITH A JAPANESE FLAIR
By Linda Sampson

     Stitches: Appliqué, satin stitch.

     Technique: All shapes appliquéd, secured and defined with satin stitch.

     Fabric: Satin on denim.

Design Source: Oriental embroidery and paintings.

BIKINI *(see color insert)*
By Anne Barnaby

     Stitches: Appliqué, satin stitch, pattern stitch.

     Technique: All shapes are appliquéd, secured and outlined with satin stitch. Pattern stitch works embellishing lines on shapes and background fabric.

     Fabric: Cotton or any appropriate material.

Design Source: Any design you like; experiment with patterned fabrics.

ZIP-POCKET CREW HAT

     Stitches: Couching, pattern stitch.

     Technique: Couching and pattern stitch used together for stitching around brim, with embroidery floss through hole in embroidery foot or held in place between toes. Work from right side. Embroidery can also start at brim and undulate or angle back and forth to the crown.

     Fabric: Heavy cotton.

Design Source: Stitch Catalog.

By Regina Bartley

chapter **10**

family crests
and monograms

Many European families—not only the nobility—have had family crests for centuries. Today, even banks and universities choose crest designs. So, why not you? Create your own tradition! You don't need a favored artist of the realm or an expensive designer, either—who could know better than you what represents the spirit of your family? Monograms and family crests are no longer an expensive luxury, and the sewing machine makes them easy to manage.

FAMILY CRESTS

The whole family should be involved in designing a crest. You may decide, for example, that tennis is your favorite game and the daisy your favorite flower; your crest design could consist of tennis rackets crossed over a daisy. Whatever the design, it should represent general family interests. Keep it simple for ease in working. Traditional crests are stylized, but your design is up to you.

The crest can be divided, with a different design in each section, or motifs can be repeated in sections or in an unbroken field. Even a simple geometric pattern can be attractive. The exterior shape can be a classic shield or an invention of your own, and you can add a brief family motto with a fine satin stitch.

Choose a three- or four-color scheme for your design. Bright red, black, green, purple, blue, silver, and gold are classic crest colors. Your family crest can be applied to clothes—a jacket lapel, a sleeve, the corner of a pocket, the top of a tie. It can decorate pillowcases, sheets, towels, or throw pillows. And it can make a wonderful wall hanging or a motif for stationery.

COUCHED DECORATIVE CREST

Stitches: Satin stitch, pattern stitch, free-surface machine embroidery, couching, applique.

Technique: Background and outlines are satin stitched, with couched and pattern-stitched accents. Designs formed with free-surface embroidery. Crest worked separately and appliqued to background fabric. Back fabric.

94

Fabric: Metallic and regular thread on silk; velvet; any suitable fabric.

Design Source: Classic family crests.

ROYAL EAGLE CREST

Stitches: Pattern stitch, varied stitch width satin stitch, satin stitch, couching, free-surface machine embroidery, appliqué.

Technique: Leaves worked with pattern stitch or varied stitch width satin stitch; borders are satin stitched. Eagles and crown couched with gold or silver Lurex, in bobbin, from reverse, using free-surface embroidery. Crest is appliquéd to pocket. Back fabric.

Fabric: Felt.

Design Source: Traditional crests, illuminated manuscripts.

MONOGRAMS

Any type of lettering can be used for monograms—block, script, old English, or anything else that appeals. A small motif—abstract, flower, bird, whatever—can also be incorporated into the design; straight stitch, zigzag, or pattern stitch can be used to border the letters.

Check your sewing machine manual for monogram patterns, and investigate patterns in fabric stores. You can also design your own letters. Draw the design first on paper and then transfer it to the fabric, using any of the transfer techniques listed in chapter 4.

The letters are then sewn, traced with satin stitch or pattern stitch or a combination of the two. Make the stitches loose or compact;

experiment first on a separate piece of fabric. Back stretch fabrics with paper or an iron-on stiffener, and hold the fabric carefully when sewing. Nonstretch fabrics can be held in a hoop, with the presser foot removed and the feed dog down. For an even line, turn the hoop to follow the contours of the letters; to change the width, move it gently sideways or up and down.

The finished monogram can be embellished with lines or figures, or incorporated into a larger design. This technique greatly expands their decorative potential. An embellished monogram can circle a sleeve, form part of the crest on a pocket, personalize a scarf— anything attractive and appropriate.

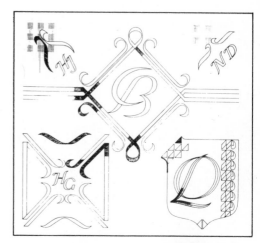

PERSONALIZED TOWELS

Stitches: Satin stitch, pattern stitch.

Technique: Straight, solid lines of letters are satin stitched; decorative lines are pattern-stitched. Back fabric.

Fabric: Cotton terrycloth.

Design Source: Stitch Catalog.

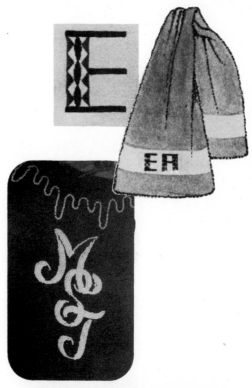

BEADED BLOUSE MONOGRAM
Courtesy Michael Futterman, New York

Stitches: Couching, free-surface machine embroidery.

Technique: Small beads are strung on nylon thread and couched in lines with free-floating method. Free-surface machine embroidery can also be used; work from reverse side with embroidery floss or fine yarn in the bobbin.

Fabric: Rayon; any appropriate material.

Design Source: Monogram patterns; Indian bead work.

NAUTICAL SHORTS
Courtesy Simplicity Pattern Company

Stitches: Pattern stitch, satin stitch.

Technique: All borders pattern-stitched, in several rows. Anchor and monogram are satin stitched, anchor with wide stitch, letters with medium, and rope with narrow stitch.

Fabric: Sharkskin; any firm fabric.

Design Source: Catalogs of marine equipment; Stitch Catalog.

S.D. AND ME
By Michael Futterman, New York

Stitches:	Varied stitch width satin stitch, free-surface machine embroidery, zigzag.
Technique:	All lines worked with varied stitch width satin stitch, with heavier lines gone over more than once. Dog's body filled in with zigzag stitch in free-surface embroidery.
Fabric:	Cotton or any suitable material, permanent press.
Design Source:	Comic books, children's books.

everything for the home

One of the most rewarding places to apply your skills and imagination in machine embroidery is your home. Every room, every corner, can be enriched with the techniques you've used so far for clothes and accessories.

PILLOWS

Many rich design possibilities exist in the embroidery work of other countries—Greece, India, Mexico, and Scandinavia are particularly noted for their embroidery art. The public library can provide excellent source material.

Any appropriate fabric can be used for pillows; check your remnants. Follow this procedure:

1. Cut fabric into a rectangle as wide as the pillow and twice as long; allow a few extra inches both ways for seams and stuffing. If you wish another shape, fold the fabric and cut, always allowing for the extra inches.

2. Embroider the fabric, generally just the front.

3. Seam three sides.

4. Insert stuffing, using an old pillow to be renovated, a ready-made muslin-covered pillow, Dacron, cotton, or kapok stuffing, or old stockings.

5. Sew up remaining seam.

6. If you want the pillow cover to be removable for washing, make an inner muslin cover for the pillow. The outside cover's fourth seam can be hemmed and closed with zippers, snaps, or Velcro, or can be made like an envelope.

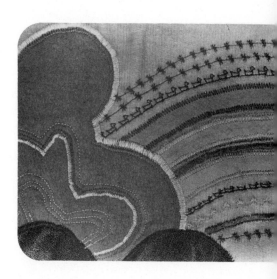

Fairway Frolic at Firefly, PILLOW, PLACEMAT, OR BEDSPREAD DETAIL
By Joan Blumenbaum

    Stitches: Straight stitch, appliqué, satin stitch, pattern stitch.

   Technique: Straight stitch used for curves at lower left; yarn in bobbin case, lines stitched from reverse side. Stitch width 1 gives a richer look to lines.

Appliqué forms all shapes; satin stitch secures and accents. Rainbow worked with various pattern stitches.

Fabric: Sturdy cotton or any appropriate material.

Design Source: Paintings of Paul Klee, Chagall, Roualt, Max Ernst.

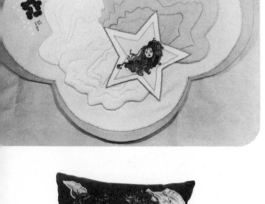

PILLOW, BEDSPREAD, OR HEADBOARD PAINTING
Fare Thee Well My Fairy Fay
By Joan Blumenbaum

Stitches: Satin stitch, appliqué, trapunto, straight stitch.

Technique: Image silk-screened on felt, then worked with various size satin stitches on darning setting, with feed cover throat plate used to facilitate easy movement of material. Stars appliquéd to each other with satin stitch; clouds appliquéd in same way to organdy backing, forming channels for trapunto. Pieces hand sewn together and outside shape outlined with braid. Sequins and beads hand sewn.

Fabric: Felt with organdy backing.

Design Source: Art nouveau.

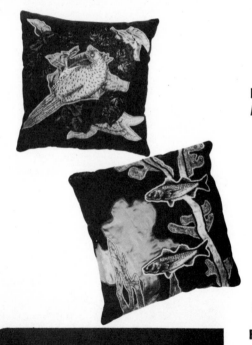

PHEASANT AND FISH PILLOWS
By Linda Sampson; photo by Bernard Lawrence

Stitches: Appliqué, satin stitch, straight stitch, couching.

Technique: Flowers, leaves, fish, and birds are all printed, richly patterned fabrics, appliquéd, secured and accented with satin stitch. Straight stitch with lighter thread adds texture and interest; couched lines are worked with embroidery floss on the surface, or from reverse side with floss in the bobbin case.

Fabric: Rayon and cotton.

Design Source: Dutch still lifes and other paintings.

FACE AND WOMAN PILLOWS
By Margaret Cusack

Stitches: Appliqué, satin stitch.

Technique: All shapes are appliquéd, secured and outlined with satin stitch. All lines worked with satin stitch.

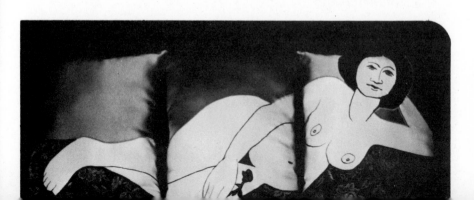

Design can be worked in parts, on separate pillows.

Fabric: Face, cotton duck; woman, satins, brocades, silks.

Design Source: Any appropriate drawing or painting.

Arabesque, PILLOW
By Linda Sampson; photo by Bernard Lawrence

Stitches: Appliqué, satin stitch.

Technique: Light shape appliquéd on dark, or vice versa; double bold line of closely stitched satin stitch highlights forms. Lines can also be stripes or diagonals.

Fabric: Cotton or any suitable material.

Design Source: Persian ceramics and minatures; cloud formations.

Desert Electrical Storm, PILLOW
By Linda Sampson; photo, Mike Sullivan

Stitches: Appliqué, satin stitch.

Technique: All shapes appliquéd, secured and accented with satin stitch. Lightning is worked in satin stitch.

Fabric: Moiré silk, velvet, printed damask, twill, felt, and cotton.

Design Source: Nature and art, landscape.

FREE-EMBROIDERED PILLOWS
By Jessica Hull Joern

Stitches: Straight stitch, free-surface machine embroidery, trapunto, Italian quilting.

Technique: Straight stitch and free-surface machine embroidery used for drawings on both pillows. Seated woman and floor worked with trapunto; chair worked with Italian quilting. Any line drawing can be adapted.

Fabric: Satin; cotton.

Design Source: Sketches; engravings.

STYLIZED PILLOW DESIGN
By Michika Sato

Stitches: Straight stitch, satin stitch, appliqué, zigzag stitch.

Technique:	Fine lines are straight stitched, heavier lines worked with satin stitch, stitch width 2. Zigzag stitch used over satin stitch to pattern it. White and black shapes are appliquéd, secured and patterned with satin and zigzag stitches. No backing required.
Fabric:	Felt.
Design Source:	Books on stylized shapes from nature; art nouveau.

OWL PILLOW
By Bucky King

Stitches:	Free-surface machine embroidery, couching, satin stitch, open-space stitch, pattern stitch.
Technique:	All lines except pattern stitch worked with free-surface embroidery. Feathers are couched over crochet cotton, eyes worked with open-space stitch. Decorative lines are pattern stitched, or can also be done with free-surface embroidery. Eyes are worked freely over machine-made bars.
Fabric:	Organdy lined with cotton.
Design Source:	Oriental paintings; nature photography.

GREEK PILLOWS
Courtesy Greek Island, New York

Stitches:	Free-surface machine embroidery, couching, satin stitch, pattern stitch.
Technique:	Free-surface machine embroidery or couching can be used for all designs; satin stitch used for lines and flowers, pattern stitch for appropriate lines in geometric-design pillow. Couch yarn for a crewel effect. Work with a hoop or back fabric.
Fabric:	Wool or wool-like synthetic, any appropriate material.
Design Source:	Folk art, in books, shops, and museums.

STYLIZED GREEK PILLOW
Courtesy Greek Island, New York

Stitches:	Free-surface machine embroidery, satin stitch, pattern stitch, couching.
Technique:	Entire design is worked with free-surface machine embroidery. Satin stitch is used for all lines; pattern stitch outlines shapes on both sides of birds and forms hulls of boats. Couching can also be used for a crewel look. Back fabric to prevent puckering.
Fabric:	Wool or similarly textured synthetic.
Design Source:	Folk art.

BEDSPREADS AND BLANKETS

FREE-FORM APPLIQUÉ
By Michika Sato

Stitches:	Appliqué, satin stitch, straight stitch, zigzag stitch.
Technique:	All shapes are appliquéd, secured and outlined with satin stitch. Straight stitch used in parallel lines as patterning; zigzag stitch used as patterning and over a narrow satin stitch to create another line quality. Shapes can also be of printed fabrics. This technique can be used for pillows, curtains, and valances as well as for bedspreads.
Fabric:	Felt or any appropriate material.
Design Source:	Nature; modern art.

GEOMETRIC BEDSPREAD FROM INDIA *(see color insert)*
Courtesy Sona, New York

Stitches:	Couching, free-surface machine embroidery.
Technique:	Couching or free-surface machine embroidery used to work the geometric square. For couching, use yarn for a crewel effect. For free-surface embroidery, work with a lightweight yarn in the bobbin case from the reverse side; for a hand-whipped look use straight stitch and stitch width 1.
Fabric:	Any appropriate material.
Design Source:	Indian and Scandinavian folk art.

BABY BLANKET SET

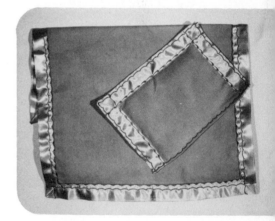

Stitches:	Pattern stitch.
Technique:	Pattern stitch used for scallops and other trim on satin edging; no backing necessary.
Fabric:	Velvet or corduroy with satin edging.
Design Source:	Stitch Catalog.

BLANKET AND PILLOWS FROM GREECE *(see color insert)*

Stitches:	Couching.
Technique:	Pillows and blanket couched with yarns to give a rich crewel work effect.
Fabric:	Wool.
Design Source:	Greek and other folk art.

BABY BLANKET AND PILLOW SET
Courtesy Simplicity Pattern Company

Stitches:	Appliqué, satin stitch, couching.
Technique:	All shapes appliquéd, secured and accented with satin stitch. Bunny face and flowers worked with satin stitch or couched. Pattern available from Simplicity.
Fabric:	Cotton or synthetic, permanent press.
Design Source:	Nursery books.

CHILD'S QUILT, Hobbie Rides Her Horse
Courtesy Simplicity Pattern Company

Stitches:	Trapunto, appliqué, couching, pattern stitch.
Technique:	All shapes appliquéd and worked with trapunto. Horse's reins, mane, and tail and hair ribbon couched. Pattern stitch can be used on clothes, for frill on underskirt, and for any other appropriate decoration. Pattern available from Simplicity.
Fabric:	Cotton or synthetic; polyester batting. Be sure all materials are machine washable and no-iron.
Design Source:	Children's books, magazines, greeting cards.

DOVE RUG OR BEDSPREAD *(see color insert)*
By Jessica Hull Joern

Stitches:	Couching, appliqué, satin stitch.
Technique:	All lines couched with heavy yarn; all shapes appliquéd, secured with satin stitch. Adjust machine for sewing through heavy layers.
Fabric:	Wool or an equivalent synthetic.
Design Source:	Posters, magazines, modern art.

QUILT WITH MATCHING PILLOWS
Courtesy Simplicity Pattern Company

Stitches:	Appliqué, satin stitch, zigzag stitch.
Technique:	All shapes appliquéd, secured with satin or zigzag stitch.
Fabric:	Cotton, preferably no-iron.
Design Source:	Quilt patterns, snowflakes, kaleidoscopes.

LINENS FOR BED AND BATH

DELICATE PILLOWCASES

Stitches:	Appliqué, satin stitch, pattern stitch, varied stitch width satin stitch.
Technique:	Butterflies and flowers are appliquéd, secured with satin stitch. Pattern stitch works lines of dots, leaves, and scalloped borders; varied stitch width satin stitch forms lines, leaves, and scallops. Free-surface machine embroidery can be used for lines. Use cotton floss in the bobbin and work from the reverse side with straight stitch, stitch width 1.
Fabric:	Fine cotton or linen.
Design Source:	Nursery books, greeting cards.

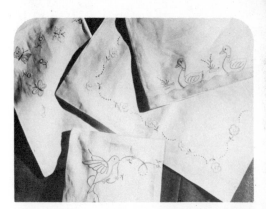

APPLIQUÉD BATH AND FINGERTIP TOWELS *(see color insert)*

Stitches:	Appliqué, satin stitch, free-surface machine embroidery, zigzag stitch.
Technique:	Appliquéd shapes are first embroidered on sheer cotton, printed fabric, or satin, then secured to towel with zigzag or satin stitch. Cut fabric larger than design, and cut away excess after securing to towel. Satin stitch accents shapes and embroiders inside lines of motifs. Free-surface machine embroidery can also be used for all designs. Use hoop or backing.
Fabric:	Terry toweling with any suitable fabric as appliqué.
Design Source:	Magazines, nature, textile designs.

GUEST TOWELS *(see color insert)*

Stitches: Free-surface machine embroidery, appliqué, satin stitch, varied stitch width satin stitch, pattern stitch.

Technique: All designs can be worked with free-surface machine embroidery. Solid color areas can be worked with appliqué, secured and accented with satin stitch. Lines worked with satin stitch, tapering lines with varied stitch width satin stitch. Pattern stitch used wherever appropriate. Use hoop or backing.

Fabric: Linen or fine cotton.

Design Source: Embroidery from Madeira and Switzerland.

EMBROIDERED APPLIQUÉ GUEST TOWELS

Stitches: Pattern stitch, satin stitch, appliqué, free-surface machine embroidery, straight stitch.

Technique: All flowers worked with forward and reverse appliqué, secured with pattern stitch. Bow and leaves worked with satin stitch, tapered in width at ends. Straight stitch also used to accent. Free-surface embroidery can be substituted for pattern stitch; use on fish. Straight stitch works fine-lined leaves in large towel's design and lines on shells. Appliquéd areas embroidered separately and then secured to towels.

Fabrics: Terrycloth; linen.

Design Source: Magazines, nature.

CURTAINS

EMBROIDERED KITCHEN CURTAINS

Stitches: Free-surface machine embroidery, zigzag stitch, couching, varied stitch width satin stitch.

Technique: Free-surface machine embroidery and zigzag fill in berries and flowers, stitch width 4. Stems and leaves also be worked in this way, with very narrow zigzag for lines. Satin stitch can also be used for lines. Floating couching technique can be used for all solid areas; scallops are worked with varied stitch width satin stitch.

Fabric: Fine cotton drip-dry or any appropriate synthetic.

Design Source: Greeting cards, children's books, wallpaper.

FLOWER PUFF KITCHEN CURTAINS

Stitches: Zigzag stitch, free-surface machine embroidery, straight stitch, couching, pattern stitch.

Technique: Zigzag stitch outlines flowers; use narrow stitch width and stitch length on flower border. Work petals with straight stitch and free-surface embroidery; small circles worked with narrow zigzag. Center puffs couched with clipped heavy yarn method; pattern stitch used for top border.

Fabric: Light cotton or a sheer.

Design Source: Seed catalogs; nature photography.

CURTAIN EMBROIDERY IDEAS

Stitches: Straight stitch, free-surface machine embroidery, cut work, satin stitch, varied stitch width satin stitch, pattern stitch.

Technique: Straight stitch used with forward-reverse technique for leaves and flowers; free-surface embroidery can also be used. Try putting embroidery floss in the bobbin and working from the reverse side, using straight stitch and stitch width 1. This technique also used to outline flowers and leaves. Cut work used to make band of small squares in center of flowers on first design, centers of flowers and leaves on second, centers of leaves and scallops of ovals on third. Satin stitch or varied stitch width satin stitch can be used instead of free-surface embroidery. Pattern stitch used to work outlines of flowers in second design, scalloped ovals and line in third.

Fabric: Organdy or voile; cotton or synthetic.

Design Source: Crewel work, lace patterns.

TABLE LINENS

SIMPLE PLACE MATS
By Loris Blake

Stitches: Appliqué, satin stitch, couching, free-surface machine embroidery, straight stitch, zigzag stitch.

Technique: Appliqué used for large white dots on first place mat, satin stitch works borders and outlines and secures applique. Pattern stitch and couching used together for all other lines, with embroidery floss placed on surface and designs worked from the right side. Free-surface embroidery and straight stitch used with couching for tulip; stem

and leaves done with straight stitch, stitch width 1. Flower filled in with zigzag. Line mats or use backing.

Fabric: Cotton or rayon polyester.

Design Source: Children's books, Stitch Catalog.

COMPANY PLACE MATS

Stitches: Pattern stitch, appliqué, free-surface machine embroidery, satin stitch.

Technique: Small leaves and flowers and dots on strawberries worked with pattern stitch; strawberries can be appliqué, secured with satin stitch, or worked with free-surface embroidery. Satin stitch and free-surface embroidery form stems and curved lines; use backing and hoop.

Fabric: Cotton, linen, or linenlike synthetic.

Design Source: Swiss and Madeira embroidery; magazines; nature books.

INDIA PLACE MAT

Stitches: Couching, satin stitch, pattern stitch, free-surface machine embroidery.

Technique: Free-floating couching with embroidery floss, or free-surface embroidery, forms everything but squares. Pattern stitch can be used as appropriate; satin stitch makes squares.

Fabric: Cotton.

Design Source: Indian embroideries, Mexican and Peruvian folk art.

THREE PLACE MATS   *(see color insert)*

Stitches: Appliqué, free-surface machine embroidery, satin stitch, pattern stitch, couching.

Technique: Appliqué or free-surface embroidery can be used for flowers on white and green mats; all other details are free-surface machine embroidery or satin stitch. Pattern stitch used for border on green mat; couching or free-surface embroidery used for blue mat.

Fabric: Linen or a linenlike synthetic.

Design Source: Swiss or Madeira embroidery.

ELEGANT NAPKINS WITH CROCHETED LACE

Stitches: Hemstitch, varied stitch width satin stitch, pattern stitch.

Technique:	Hemstitch used to work straight embroidered lines, varied stitch width satin stitch for rest of design. Pattern stitch can also be used for formal design. Lace can be omitted; tablecloth or place mats can be done in the same manner.
Fabric:	Linen or linenlike rayon polyester.
Design Source:	Old linens; merchandise in fine linen shops.

TURKISH FRINGED TABLECLOTH

Stitches:	Free-surface machine embroidery, straight stitch.
Technique:	Free-surface embroidery and straight stitch used together with embroidery floss in the bobbin; work from reverse side. Use a hoop to keep work flat. Thread is metal floss.
Fabric:	Cotton, linen, or linenlike synthetic.
Design Source:	Turkish embroidery.

FAGOTED TABLECLOTH

Stitches:	Fagoting, straight stitch, open-space stitching.
Technique:	Join two lengths of fine tape with fagoting, using tailor-tacking foot, or buy a piece of tape that is adaptable to this effect. Pin tape in position and straight stitch lengths together as you go. Place looped tape in a hoop and work with open-space stitching for web effect, varying designs to please yourself. For loops close to the edge, baste to a strip of fabric to secure in a hoop; remove fabric after web is finished. Stitch the whole looped and webbed design to a corner of a tablecloth and cut away the excess fabric underneath. This technique can also be used for curtains, pillowcases, or pillows.
Fabric:	Fine linen or cotton.
Design Source:	Iron grille work; old English designs.

TABLE RUNNER OR WALL HANGING
By Jan Eisenman

Stitches:	Appliqué, satin stitch.
Technique:	All shapes are ready-made eyelet embroidery, appliquéd, secured with satin stitch. Any pleasantly textured fabric can be used, in any design.
Fabric:	Linen.
Design Source:	Modern art; your environment.

PERSIAN TABLECLOTH

Stitches:	Hemstitch, couching.
Technique:	Hemstitch used for all large leaves and flower shapes. All lines, small leaves and flowers, and borders around larger shapes are couched with surface or bobbin technique. Use a single hemstitch needle for fine fabrics and a double one for heavier materials. This technique can also be used for corners and centers of tablecloth, pillows, bedspreads, and draperies.
Fabric:	Cotton.
Design Source:	Persian ceramics, embroidery, and miniatures.

OPENWORK TABLECLOTH *(see color insert)*
By Bucky King

Stitches:	Free-surface machine embroidery, cut work, pattern stitch, satin stitch.
Technique:	Free-surface machine embroidery used for all but center spoked design. Fabric cut out inside triangles of spokes, or pattern stitch used on all but center. Satin stitch outlines spokes in center, then outlines cut work.
Fabric:	Organdy; linen, cotton, or synthetic. Keep fabric care in mind.
Design Source:	Loosely woven textiles; carved furniture; wrought iron.

CREWEL TABLECLOTH FROM INDIA
Courtesy Sona, New York

Stitches:	Couching, free-surface machine embroidery, zigzag stitch.
Technique:	All heavier lines couched for crewel look. Free-surface embroidery used for all fine lines; use yarn in bobbin, stitch width 1, with straight stitch, or couch a fine yarn. Use zigzag with free-surface embroidery where indicated in the pattern. This technique can also be used for a bedspread.
Fabric:	Sturdy, somewhat rough-weave cotton.
Design Source:	Indian and Persian art and folk art.

GREEK TABLE RUNNER
Courtesy Greek Island, New York

Stitches:	Couching, free-surface machine embroidery, pattern stitch, satin stitch.

Technique: Entire design can be worked with couching or free-surface embroidery. Much of design uses automatic pattern shapes, and all lines can easily be satin stitched. Work from reverse side with yarn in the bobbin case for an embossed finish. Back fabric if you work from the right side.

Fabric: Wool or any appropriate material.

Design Source: Folk art of various countries.

APPLIQUÉD TABLECLOTH
Courtesy Simplicity Pattern Company

Stitches: Appliqué, satin stitch.

Technique: All shapes are appliquéd, secured with satin stitch. Appliqués can also be embellished with pattern stitch.

Fabric: Cotton or synthetic.

Design Source: Snowflakes; kaleidoscopes; geometry.

FURNITURE AND UPHOLSTERY

ANTIQUE CHAIR BACK

Stitches: Couching, free-surface machine embroidery, trapunto.

Technique: Bands surrounding cheetah and falcon are embroidery floss attached with floating surface couching. All outlines are couched with floss or cord in the bobbin, worked from reverse side. Head and tail of the falcon and entire cheetah, plus designs over their heads, are filled in with free-surface embroidery. Trapunto used to pad falcon and cheetah; use Dacron or cotton for best results. A simpler, more contemporary design can also be worked in this manner, with one end left open to slip over a chair back.

Fabric:	Cotton, linen, or a synthetic.
Design Source:	Renaissance interior designs and tapestries.

LANDSCAPE COUCHES
By Michelle Clifton

Stitches:	Trapunto.
Technique:	Rainbow and Palm Tree couches are built up of padded forms, all trapunto. Clouds form arm rests on rainbow couch. Palm tree couch built over conventional frame, with bushes as arm rests. Any landscape can be adapted.
Fabric:	Felt, vinyl, knits; leather.
Design Source:	Children's books; art nouveau; landscape.

TRAPUNTO ART COUCHES
By Michelle Clifton

Stitches:	Trapunto.
Technique:	New York City couch and Love Seat are built of padded forms, all trapunto. New York couch has Empire State and Chrysler Buildings; arm rests are Brooklyn and George Washington Bridges. Statue of Liberty pillow rests on waves of seat. Love Seat is all hearts, built over a conventional love seat.
Fabric:	Felt (New York), vinyl, leather; satin (Love Seat).
Design Source:	Any cityscape. Love Seat, Victorian novels.

toys and more

Making fun, safe, imaginative toys requires little money and less time. Better still, involve a child in the planning and you'll find an inspiring, inventive helper. Discuss what to make and draw your design ideas together—you'll enjoy it as much as your helper will.

Before you start sewing, keep these hints in mind:

1. Use sturdy, washable, colorfast fabrics.

2. Stuffing, when needed, should also be washable.

3. Bits of fabric (stockings, sheets, scraps) are adequate for stuffing; shredded foam rubber is better. Dacron-cotton or polyester batting is best for smaller objects.

4. Determine softness or firmness needed in stuffing, and choose accordingly.

5. Always embroider the parts of an object before joining them into a whole.

6. Leave a big enough opening for easy stuffing, then close the final seam.

7. A pipe cleaner inside a tail or an ear before stuffing will make it stand up or curl.

8. Fill out curves and corners as you stuff with a pencil, an orange stick, or a crochet hook.

ANIMAL PILLOWS

GIANT TURTLE

Stitches: Couching.

Technique: All lines are drawn on the back of a roughly turtle-shaped pillow; then bulky yarn is couched by placing the yarn between the presser foot toes. For easy handling, work from the center out; hang yarn ball in a shopping bag on chair. Bottom and top of the turtle are stitched together, leaving an opening for insertion of pillow. Close the opening with a zipper. This technique can also be used for a giant flower or curled-up cat pillow.

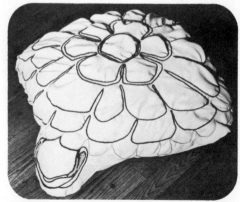

By Regina Bartley

Fabric: Heavy permanent press cotton; durable vinyl.

Design Source: Children's books; animal and reptile books.

OWL TWICE AS WISE

Stitches: Appliqué, satin stitch, varied stitch width satin stitch, pattern stitch.

Technique: Eyes and beak are appliquéd, secured with satin stitch and decorated with pattern stitch. Feather lines are varied stitch width satin stitch. Embroidered fabric is sewed together and tassels are added as decoration. Any animal can be adapted.

Fabric: Heavy cotton.

Design Source: Nursery books, greeting cards, posters.

STUFFED TOYS

DANGLY LEGS

Stitches: Couching, appliqué.

Technique: Hair on head and lines around eyes are couched with textured yarn. Features are appliqué, attached with fabric glue. Doll is a stuffed cube; legs are stuffed tubes stitched to body.

Fabric: Cotton; features, felt.

Design Source: Nursery characters, fantasy, children's books.

ANIMALS FROM INDIA *(see color insert)*
Courtesy Sona, New York

Stitches: Free-surface machine embroidery, appliqué, satin stitch, pattern stitch.

Technique: Free-surface machine embroidery used for all designs on horse and bell. Bird's wing, tail, and beak appliquéd, secured where necessary with satin stitch. Wings are decorated with pattern stitch. Stitch before assembling parts and stuffing.

Fabric: Cotton.

Design Source: Indian art and folk art.

STUFFED PIG AND LION

Stitches: Appliqué, satin stitch, couching, pattern stitch.

Technique: Features and flowers are appliqué, secured with tacking and satin stitch. Satin stitch used for pig's face and lion's eyes; lion's mane and tail are couched. Pattern stitch can be used on eyes, flowers, and leaves of pig.

Fabric: Cotton (pig); knit (lion).

Design Source: Nursery tales and children's books.

PAJAMA OR TOWEL BAG
Courtesy Simplicity Pattern Company

Stitches: Satin stitch, couching, pattern stitch, appliqué.

Technique: Lines of face worked with satin stitch; tooth is appliqué; hair is couched. Pattern stitch can be used on the pocket, down the front, or on the ears. Stuff the head after it is stitched and ears are added. Any animal can be adapted, and floppy paws can be added.

Fabric: No-iron cotton or synthetic.

Design Source: Children's books, greeting cards, children's drawings.

LOBSTER BEANBAG

Stitches: Pattern stitch, couching.

Technique: Scales on tail are pattern stitched, embroidered after lobster was stuffed with beans for a padded effect between some pattern stitch rows. Eyes are couched before stuffing with clipped heavy yarn. Any animal shape can be adapted.

Fabric: Sturdy no-iron cotton or synthetic.

Design Source: Children's books, greeting cards.

CLOTH BLOCKS

Stitches: Appliqué, pattern stitch, satin stitch.

Technique: Six sides of block are appliquéd with white fabric; outlines are pattern stitched. Satin stitch used to secure and accent shapes, and for detail work.

Fabric: Washable, no-iron cotton or synthetic; vinyl.

Design Source: Children's books, greeting cards, wallpaper.

DOLLS

PEASANT LADY
Courtesy The Gazebo, New York

Stitches: Satin stitch, couching.

Technique: Satin stitch used to work features and outline shapes; hair is couched. Doll is stitched together like a pillow and stuffed after embroidery.

Fabric: Any scraps of washable fabric.

Design Source: Books on dolls.

By Regina Bartley

HATTED DOLL

Stitches: Appliqué, pattern stitch, couching.

Technique: All surface shapes, eyes, mouth, and flowers, are appliquéd, secured and decorated with pattern stitch. Flowers are stitched only at centers. Cap is decorated with couched yarn. Hat is separate, and can be removed; head has a long forehead that fits into hat. Doll is made like a pillow, stitched together after embroidery.

Fabric: Cotton body and face; felt hat and appliqué; yarn for pompons and cheeks.

Design Source: Children's books, children's drawings.

"HOBBY" DOLL (facing page)
Courtesy Simplicity Pattern Company

Stitches: Satin stitch, couching, appliqué, pattern stitch.

Technique: Hatband and bow and all lines on dress, face, and bonnet are satin stitch; eyes, dots on dress, and bonnet design are pattern stitch. Basket is couched ribbon; cat and feet are appliqué, secured with satin stitch. Doll is embroidered first, then sewn together and stuffed.

Fabric: Cotton or anything washable.

Design Source: Doll books, children's books.

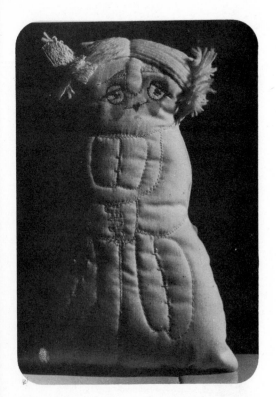

LITTLE LADY
Courtesy The Gazebo, New York

Stitches: Zigzag stitch, varied stitch width satin stitch, free-surface machine embroidery, straight stitch, trapunto, couching.

Technique: Zigzag stitch outlines face, arms, hands, and eyes; straight stitch outlines other forms of body, nose, and mouth. Eyebrows are worked with varied stitch width satin stitch, mouth with free-surface embroidery. Body quilted with trapunto, and hair couched. Doll is made like a pillow.

Fabric: Unbleached muslin.

Design Source: Characters from children's books; cloud formations.

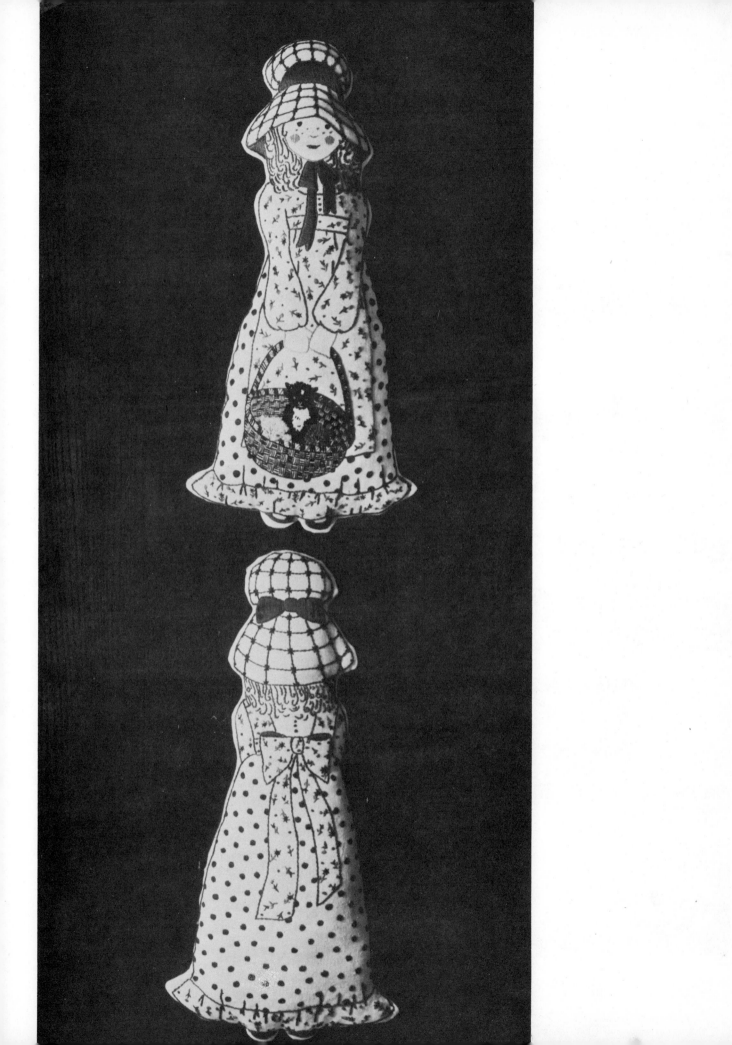

WALL HANGINGS

Medieval Lion, APPLIQUÉD COLLAGE
By Margaret Cusack

Stitches:	Appliqué, varied stitch width satin stitch.
Technique:	Lion is appliquéd, outlined and detailed with varied stitch width satin stitch. Tail can be attached separately, hanging free or stiffened with fine wire or a pipe cleaner.
Fabric:	No-iron synthetic; corduroy.
Design Source:	Animal books and posters.

AFRICAN-INSPIRED BIRD HANGINGS *(see color insert)*

Stitches:	Appliqué, satin stitch, straight stitch, free-surface machine embroidery.
Technique:	All shapes appliquéd, secured and outlined with satin stitch. Large shapes sewed first. Straight stitch forms lines inside wings, neck, and tail of eagle; free-surface embroidery used to work breast.
Fabric:	Cotton.
Design Source:	African arts.

INDIAN ANIMAL BANNERS
Courtesy Sona, New York

Stitches:	Free-surface machine embroidery, appliqué, satin stitch.
Technique:	Entire design can be worked with free-surface machine embroidery, or shapes can be appliquéd, and excess cut away. Satin stitch can be used for lines with free-surface embroidery, and is used to secure appliquéd shapes. Use embroidery floss in the bobbin and work with straight stitch width 1. Borders can be pattern stitched or couched.
Fabric:	Cotton.
Design Source:	Indian folk art.

APPLIQUÉ WALL HANGINGS
By Stephanie Natta

Stitches:	Appliqué, satin stitch, couching.
Technique:	All shapes appliquéd, secured and accented with satin stitch. All line details worked with satin stitch; cat's whiskers couched. Pattern stitch can be used wherever wanted.
Fabric:	Cotton, felt, silk, velvet, any scraps.
Design Source:	Magazines, greeting cards; crewel designs.

Embroidered appliqué for little girls.

Appliquéd rompers.

Jackets, free-surface embroidery.

Jeans suit with Mexican flair. *Courtesy Fred Leighton, New York.*

Mexican dress. *Courtesy Fred Leighton, New York.*

Child's appliquéd tops.

Shirtwaist dress. *Courtesy Simplicity Pattern Company.*

Embroidered leather boots.

Oriental caftan. *Courtesy American-Israeli Cultural Center.*

Pattern-stitched suit. *Courtesy Simplicity Pattern Company.*

Fringed-neckline jersey. *Courtesy Simplicity Pattern Company.*

Oriental caftan. *Courtesy American-Israeli Cultural Center.*

Pattern-stitched suit. *Courtesy Simplicity Pattern Company.*

Velvet and gold evening bag.

Embroidered and appliquéd caftan. *Courtesy American-Israeli Cultural Center.*

Embroidered cape. *Courtesy Simplicity Pattern Company.*

Satin stitched and couched peasant designs for night-gown and blouses.

Appliquéd collage wall hanging. *Shulimit Litan; courtesy American-Israeli Cultural Center.*

Embroidered cape. *Courtesy Simplicity Pattern Company.*

Pattern stitching edges sleeves of velvet evening jacket.

Caftan.

Open-space embroidered silk scarf.

Gold pattern stitch and appliqué on evening wrap.

Oriental caftan. *Courtesy American-Israeli Cultural Center.*

Indian-design bedspread or tablecloth. *Courtesy Sona, New York.*

Couched blanket and pillows from Greece. *Courtesy Greek Island, New York.*

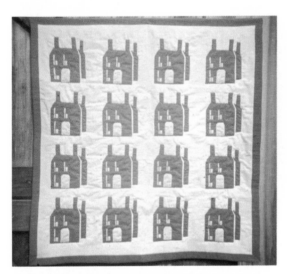

Appliquéd quilt. *Jan Eisenman.*

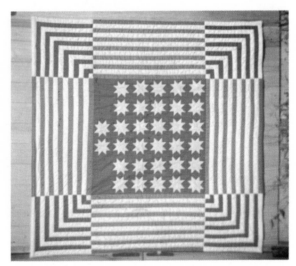

Appliquéd quilt. *Jan Eisenman.*

Geometric embroidery from India. *Courtesy Sona, New York.*

Couched pillow from Greece. *Courtesy Greek Island, New York.*

Appliqué designs for fingertip towels.

Animal toys, ladies' bags, and appliquéd hanging cone from India. *Courtesy Sona, New York.*

Anteater banner from India. *Courtesy Sona, New York.*

Placemats with appliqué, couching, pattern stitching, and free-surface embroidery.

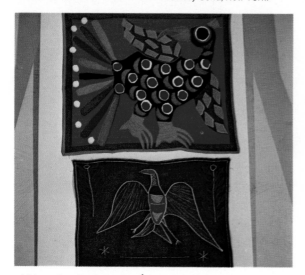

African-inspired appliqué hangings, peacock and eagle.

Bath towels with appliqué, pattern stitching, and free-surface embroidery.

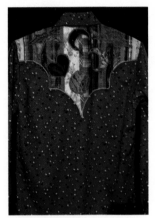

Men's shirt with appliqué. *Anne Barnaby.*

Bikini, side. *Anne Barnaby.*

Jazzy jeans, detail. *Linda Sampson; photo, Jay Good.*

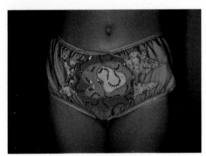

Bikini, front. *Anne Barnaby.*

Love Stars Vibrations, velvet vest.

Birds, Flowers, and Butterfly, shorts. *Linda Sampson; photo, Vince Aiosa.*

American flag bag. *Jeanette Feldman.*

Fantasy from India, embroidered appliqué slacks.

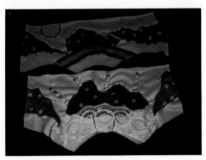

Embroidered shorts. *Anne Barnaby.*

Red-on-red mohair pillow.

Tablecloth, cut work and free-surface embroidery. *Bucky King.*

Christmas banner.
Jan Eisenman.

Satin trapunto pillow. *Jessica Hull Joern.*

Couched and appliquéd dove rug.
Jessica Hull Joern.

Pattern-stitched blanket.

Appliquéd kneeler. *Bucky King.*

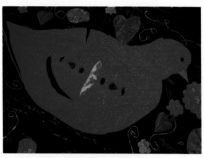

Couched and appliquéd dove rug detail.
Jessica Hull Joern.

Satin-stitched head-
board, detail.

Spaghetti, appliquéd collage. *Margaret Cusack*.

Untitled—chess player, soft sculpture. *Sidney Blum*.

Shortcake, appliquéd collage. *Margaret Cusack*.

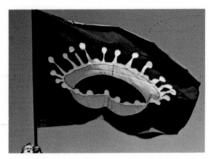

Royal Flag, abstract appliquéd banner. *Anders Holmquist*.

Joy with Machine Embroidery, yarn painting. *Regina Bartley*.

Midnight Rainbow—Morning Starshine, detail. *Joan A. Blumenbaum*.

Flag, abstract appliquéd banner. *Anders Holmquist*.

Abstract, appliqué painting, detail. *Linda Waddington*.

Midnight Rainbow—Morning Starshine, soft sculpture. *Joan A. Blumenbaum*.

Whip-Poor-Will, BANNER
By Jan Eisenman

      Stitches: Appliqué, straight stitch, pattern stitch.

  Technique: All shapes are appliquéd, secured with straight stitch. Pattern stitch can be used to emphasize feathers. Button forms eye.

       Fabric: Cotton, linen; wool; anything with interesting textures and patterns.

Design Source: Nature books.

Just Ducky, APPLIQUÉ

      Stitches: Appliqué, couching.

  Technique: All shapes are appliquéd. Heavy outlines are surface couched with bulky yarn or soft cord between presser foot toes.

       Fabric: Linen, rayon, polyester, burlap; any available scraps.

Design Source: Children's books, flower books, fish books.

TREE BANNER
By Jan Eisenman

      Stitches: Couching.

  Technique: Entire design couched with sheepskin strips, with fur clipped away at intervals to form short fuzzy lines of design.

       Fabric: Linen background; sheepskin strips.

Design Source: Greeting cards, textile design, iron grille work.

Child's Drawing, APPLIQUÉ
By Judith Spencer Levy

>| | |
>|---|---|
>| *Stitches:* | Appliqué, satin stitch, couching, pattern stitch. |
>| *Technique:* | All shapes are appliquéd, secured and accented with satin stitch. All line details are satin stitched. Hair is couched; pattern stitch can be used as desired. |
>| *Fabric:* | Cotton, linen; any suitable material. |
>| *Design Source:* | Children's drawings. |

Victorian Houses, BANNER
By Jan Eisenman

>| | |
>|---|---|
>| *Stitches:* | Appliqué, satin stitch, couching. |
>| *Technique:* | All shapes are appliquéd, secured with satin stitch. All lines are couched; note line of couched dilly balls. Flag is partially free. |
>| *Fabric:* | Felt. |
>| *Design Source:* | Old houses; old photographs. |

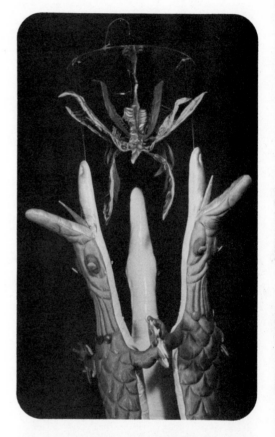

Crocodile, SOFT SCULPTURE
By Priscilla Kepner Sage

>| | |
>|---|---|
>| *Stitches:* | Trapunto, satin stitch. |
>| *Technique:* | Trapunto used for designs on backs and heads and bird above mouths. Satin stitch used for trapunto and for attaching pieces. Stuff after embroidering, then hang. |
>| *Fabric:* | Double-knit stretch and vinyl. |
>| *Design Source:* | Books on animals, insects, butterflies, etc. |

GATHERING FOR A MOBILE

>| | |
>|---|---|
>| *Stitches:* | Pattern stitch, satin stitch. |
>| *Technique:* | All shapes cut and then embroidered. Some shapes stuffed and decorated with pattern stitch; satin stitch secures, accents, and decorates other shapes. |
>| *Fabric:* | Velvet, silk, rayon, wool; a variety of textures. |
>| *Design Source:* | Children's books. |

new clothes for old: recycling

Who doesn't have at least one dress or shirt or pair of pants that's not quite right, but too good to dispose of? A little time and effort, and you can embroider new life into hand-me-downs and back-of-the-closet rejects.

LENGTHENING OR ENLARGING

To lengthen a coat, skirt, or dress, if a matching fabric is unavailable, choose a fabric that coordinates well with your garment. Cut a strip of fabric, allowing extra width for hem and seam; let down the old hem and join the strip at the bottom edge of the garment with a straight stitch seam. The next step is the fun one—embroider over the line that marks the old hem, over the new stitch line. The embroidery can be left at that or expanded into a border design.

To enlarge, follow the same procedure with vertical seams; buttons can be removed and replaced on the newly embroidered strip. Or open the side seams and insert a triangular piece of fabric.

REVERSING

Often a seemingly worn-out coat or jacket can be turned inside out and reseamed; the fabric on the inside, having received less wear, will look fresh and new. It's easy to do—just open up all the seams, reverse all the parts, and reseam, inside out. Embroider the new seams with a handsome machine pattern stitch.

LENGTHENING AND SHORTENING SLEEVES

The procedure for lengthening or shortening sleeves is much as described for lengthening a dress. To lengthen short sleeves, add a straight tubular section; or add a flared, gathered, or cuffed sleeve section. Long sleeves can be cut to the desired length, allowing for hem or cuff; they can be flared, pointed, or scalloped. Machine embroidery over an old seam line or on a new cuff will change the look of the garment entirely.

STRAIGHTENING PLEATED SKIRTS

A pleated skirt you're tired of can be straightened with embroidery. Pin the pleats together; if they are very narrow, try skipping one or two every three or so pleats. Stitch them together with an attractive pattern stitch, and cut the extra fabric from underneath. Try stitching only partway down the pleats; you may prefer that effect.

SALVAGING FRAYED COLLARS AND CUFFS

Old shirts can be restored to life with matching fabric, or given a whole new look with a contrasting material. Cut the collar off just above the joining seam. Cut the cuffs off *only* if they fold back, also at the joining seam. Cut your new fabric into three strips, one as long as the neckline of the shirt and two as long as the wristline, allowing for seams. The width of the strips should be about three or four inches. Place the right side of the fabric strips against the right side of the shirt neck and wrist lines, and seam together. Stitch the ends together, tuck in raw edges, and stitch. Embroider with a machine pattern stitch all around the edges of the collar and cuffs.

POCKETS AND PATCHES

Pockets can be used to perk up just about anything one can wear, and you can machine embroider a pocket to suit every mood and garment. Patches are more utilitarian but no less fun—they can do wonders for a tired shirt or pair of pants. Try embroidering them in any shape and size, in every color. Any of the designs in the Denims chapter can be well adapted to patches.

chapter 14

the decorative wall

Imaginative, colorful banners can do a lot to brighten a dull room, and they cost almost nothing if you use scraps and remnants. You'll find yourself developing a new way of looking at the world.

TECHNICAL HINTS

METHODS OF HANGING

Hem the top of your work one inch wide or more; insert a dowel, a spindle, or a drapery or metal rod. Or make hanging tabs, strips folded over and stitched at both ends to the top edge of your embroidery. These strips can also be a continuation of the embroidery, folded over at one end to the top edge. Dowels, spindles, or metal or drapery rods are then inserted.

METHODS OF WEIGHTING

Lightweight fabrics don't hang well by themselves. Use dressmaker's weights on the lower edge of the embroidery, or hang a dowel or rod at the bottom. Wall hangings can also be stretched like paintings.

DECORATIVE TOUCHES

Anything appropriate can help give your embroidery a finished look. Try tassels at the ends of the rod or on the bottom, finials on the supporting rods, or fringes, macrame, or beading on the bottom. Feathers, fur, or any other unusual material can also add distinction—use your imagination.

SEWN PAINTINGS AND DRAWINGS

House with Rainbow, APPLIQUÉD COLLAGE
By Margaret Cusack

  Stitches: Appliqué, satin stitch, couching, free-surface machine embroidery, pattern stitch.

  Technique: Large fabric areas are appliquéd; all outlines are satin stitched. Couched yarn can be substituted for satin stitch to enrich root, tree, and house

outlines, and leaflike lines on tree. Flowers can be varicolored couched yarns. Rainbow can be appliquéd with strips of velvet or felt or done by free-surface machine embroidery. The windows can be appliquéd lace or pattern stitch on sheer fabric.

Fabric:	Rich brocades, velvet, felt, tweeds, and lace.
Design Source:	Photographs of your own home; any attractive house.

CHARLIE CHAPLIN PORTRAIT
By Margaret Cusack

Stitches:	Appliqué, satin stitch, free-surface machine embroidery, pattern stitch.
Technique:	Figure and violin are appliquéd, secured and accented with satin stitch. Free-surface machine embroidery can be used for face instead of appliqué. The background can be pattern stitches on solid fabric rather than tweed.
Fabric:	Cotton, felt, wool.
Design Source:	Storybooks, album covers.

King of Textiles, COLLAGE (DETAIL)
By Dianne Koppisch King; photo by David Chamberlain

Stitches:	Appliqué, satin stitch.
Technique:	All shapes appliquéd, secured and accented with satin stitch. Sharp emphasis on contrasting lights and darks gives additional strength. Colors are very rich.
Fabric:	Felt, rayon, cotton, corduroy.
Design Source:	Art books, church windows, stained glass.

Circus, COLLAGE
By Margaret Cusack

Stitches:	Appliqué, satin stitch, couching.
Technique:	All areas except reins are appliquéd, secured and accented with satin stitch. Reins are couched, stitched only at contact points. Add pattern stitch for interest.
Fabric:	Any richly textured and patterned material.
Design Source:	Circus posters, children's books.

FOOD AS COLLAGE: Beef Kebabs, Asparagus Hollandaise
By Margaret Cusack

Stitches: Appliqué, satin stitch, varied stitch width satin stitch.

Technique: All shapes are appliquéd, secured and accented with satin stitch. Asparagus textured with satin stitch; beef kebabs accented with varied stitch width satin stitch. Pattern stitch can decorate dish; Shadow is satin stitching on net.

Fabric: *Beef Kebabs,* crepe and silk, velvet, and linen; *Asparagus,* pattern weave, piqué, and cotton duck or linen.

Design Source: Any food; illustrations in magazines and cookbooks. Appeared in *Esquire* magazine.

Siena Square, APPLIQUÉ
By Jan Eisenman

> *Stitches:* Appliqué, satin stitch.
>
> *Technique:* Appliqué used for all shapes, stitched down and then trimmed. Satin stitch, in same color as fabric, secures shapes.
>
> *Fabric:* Felt, cotton; any interestingly textured or patterned material.
>
> *Design Source:* Travel posters; magazine pictures; photographs.

After the Fall, APPLIQUÉD PAINTING
By Judith Schoener

> *Stitches:* Appliqué, satin stitch.
>
> *Technique:* All shapes appliquéd, secured with satin stitch and then trimmed. Broad design structure is established first, then developed in greater detail, using many overlays of fabric.
>
> *Fabric:* Cotton.
>
> *Design Source:* Art books; semiabstract paintings.

Candlelight, COLLAGE
By Jettee Penraat

> *Stitches:* Appliqué, straight stitch, double-needle stitching, zigzag stitch.
>
> *Technique:* Candles are appliquéd, secured with zigzag stitch. Straight stitch used to enhance flames. Iron-on Pellon on longest candle applied without added stitching. Candles stitched with double needle for raised vertical lines.
>
> *Fabric:* Silk, gauze, satin, felt, and cotton on soft satin.
>
> *Design Source:* Greeting cards. From UNICEF "Festival of Lights" cards.

MARILYN PORTRAIT
By Margaret Cusack

  Stitches: Appliqué, satin stitch, pattern stitch.

 Technique: All fabric areas are appliquéd, secured with satin stitch. Face drawn on background, with shadow areas overlaid on light areas. Satin stitch accents hair rhythms and nose; decorative touches can be pattern stitched. Rhinestones used for earrings.

   Fabric: Silk, satin, felt; rhinestones.

Design Source: Photographs, magazines, newspapers, posters.

WALL HANGINGS

Persian Banquet, 7′ 5½″ x 4′ 6″
By Norman Laliberte; courtesy Arras Gallery, New York

  Stitches: Free-surface machine embroidery, pattern stitch, appliqué, reverse appliqué.

 Technique: Designs on border, table, and figures stitched first with free-surface machine embroidery; pattern stitches can also be used. Embroidered shapes are appliquéd to background. Diamonds with spoked circle design are worked with reverse appliqué. Overall effect of richness is greatly enhanced by simplicity of the background; design is held together by strong border design. Designs can also be couched with embroidery floss. Back fabric.

   Fabric: Cotton and felt; silk and velvet.

Design Source: Paintings; any grouping of people, houses, birds, flowers, abstract shapes, etc.

Lady on Brown Background
By Michika Sato

    Stitches: Appliqué, reverse appliqué, zigzag stitch, satin stitch, pattern stitch.

    Technique: Black, blue, and white fabric layers stitched and cut away in reverse appliqué to achieve design. Leaves are appliquéd. All appliqué trimmed after stitching, secured with zigzag stitch and finished and accented with narrow satin stitch. Pattern stitch used in and around leaves to enrich design.

    Fabric: Cotton.

    Design Source: Folk art of all countries.

APPLIQUÉD COLLAGE WALL HANGING
By Shulimit Litan; courtesy American-Israeli Cultural Center, New York

    Stitches: Appliqué, satin stitch.

    Technique: All shapes are appliquéd, secured with narrow satin stitch.

    Fabric: Felt on lightly textured linen or cotton.

    Design Source: Iron grille work; Moorish and Persian art.

CHRISTMAS ALPHABET
By Margaret Cusack

    Stitches: Appliqué, satin stitch, varied stitch width satin stitch.

    Technique: Letters and shapes appliquéd, secured with satin stitch; stem details added with varied stitch width satin stitch.

    Fabric: Linen with satin.

    Design Source: Old English lettering. From *The Reader's Digest Book of Christmas.*

Ascension Balloon, HANGING
By Jan Eisenman

    Stitches: Appliqué, straight stitch, couching.

    Technique: Basket is appliquéd and horizontal and vertical lines worked with straight stitch. Sheepskin strips are couched; fur is clipped at intervals to form designs.

    Fabric: Linen; denim.

    Design Source: Plant life, fish shapes, abstract art.

Blue Barns, COUCHED APPLIQUÉ *(facing page)*
By Jan Eisenman

> *Stitches:* Appliqué, couching, straight stitch.
>
> *Technique:* Barns and sky are appliquéd; tree forms are couched. Straight stitch used for linear interest on and around trees. Birds in cage, children behind gate, or flowers seen through iron rail can also be adapted.
>
> *Fabric:* Linen, wool, felt; various textured fabrics. Experiment with tearing for edge interest.
>
> *Design Source:* Nature, magazines, photographs.

WALL HANGING IN BAS-RELIEF
By Deanna Glad

> *Stitches:* Trapunto, appliqué, satin stitch.
>
> *Technique:* All shapes are appliquéd; sun, cows, bull, and apples worked with trapunto. Satin stitch used to secure shapes; horns and face of bull do not touch background.
>
> *Fabric:* Cotton, felt, and corduroy.
>
> *Design Source:* Animal forms; African and Eskimo art.

Chisos, BANNER
By Jeanette Feldman

> *Stitches:* Satin stitch, straight stitch, trapunto, appliqué, couching.
>
> *Technique:* Vinyl and satin forms are appliquéd, secured with satin stitch. Straight stitch forms free-form lines inside circle; trapunto used on vinyl and inside of circle. Lines surrounding circle are couched with satin stitch.
>
> *Fabric:* Shiny vinyl and satin on wool.
>
> *Design Source:* Sculptured reliefs in museums and galleries.

COUCHED HANGING, On an Afternoon in November
By Jeanette Feldman

> *Stitches:* Couching, appliqué, satin stitch.
>
> *Technique:* All shapes are appliquéd. Heavier lines of yarn are couched, surface couching in some areas and free floating couching in others. Fringes formed by leaving ends of the couched yarns free and adding other strands of yarn. Satin stitch secures appliqué and creates more subtle lines of textures within shapes.
>
> *Fabric:* Crinkled vinyl, suede, moiré silk, and velvet.
>
> *Design Source:* Textural contrasts in nature.

Open, BANNER
By Jan Eisenman

Stitches: Appliqué, satin stitch.

Technique: All shapes are appliquéd, secured with satin stitch, stitched down first and then trimmed. Raw edges finished with satin stitch.

Fabric: Linen and cotton.

Design Source: Any message; monograms; books on lettering.

King, Queen, and Castle, QUILT HANGING
By Elizabeth Gurrier; photograph by Robert Raiche

Stitches: Trapunto, double-needle stitching, straight stitch, pattern stitch.

Technique: Most quilted areas are worked with trapunto; double-needle straight stitch over light padding can achieve finer quilting designs. Pattern stitch can also be used with long stitch length for finely quilted areas. Faces are hand embroidered.

Fabric: Cotton.

Design Source: Illuminated manuscripts, children's books; paintings of castles or cathedrals.

contemporary machine embroidery: a new art form

The techniques of surface enrichment of fabrics are being applied by creative artists in new and fascinating ways. Galleries and museums in the United States and around the world exhibit machine embroideries; many fabric artists have won awards for the excellence and originality of their works. The Smithsonian Institution in Washington, D.C., has chosen machine embroidery art for its permanent collection. And embroidery art is now taught by artists in many colleges and universities.

The sense of discovery and enthusiasm in working with this new art can set fire to your own creative impulses. You can work three-dimensionally, making soft sculptures with machine embroidery. You can stretch, form, and mold threads with this contemporary tool, turning machine embroidery into lacy, airy, open forms that float and soar, casting beautiful, ever-changing shadows. You can apply embroidery to fabric as a painter applies oil to canvas, combine stitched lines with layered fabrics, glazing color on color or achieving handsome collage.

The sewing machine is a tool, as are the potter's wheel and the sculptor's mallet. And as a tool, it presents you with a whole new world of possibilities. Don't limit yourself to conventional backgrounds; experiment with unexpected materials like raffia, plastics, fine aluminum wire, and screening. The fine art of portraiture can be achieved through the versatility of appliqué and machine stitchery. And you can make your own unique and various jewelry.

Your creations, in short, can be as varied as your moods and personality. To get your imagination and your creativity started, the following examples include a selection of works from artists all over the country.

HANGINGS

FACE QUILT
By Elizabeth S. Gurrier

> *Technique:* Pattern stitch over light padding backed with soft fabric. Double needle can be used. Faces hand embroidered.

SEA LACERY
By Everett K. Sturgeon; photo by Grover Gilchrist

> *Technique:* Open-space embroidery with extended webs and tassels.

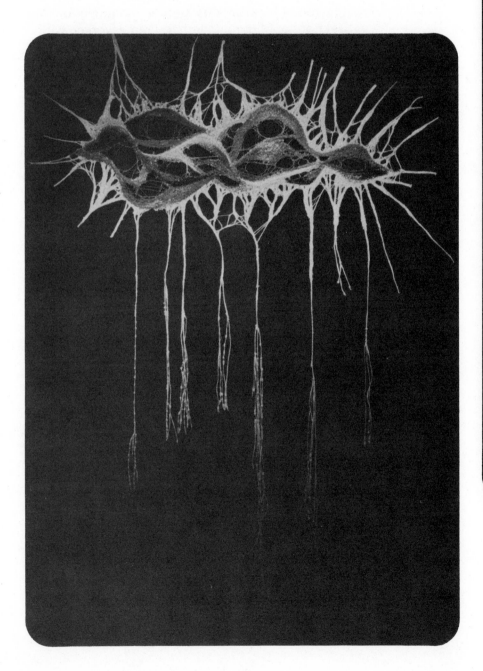

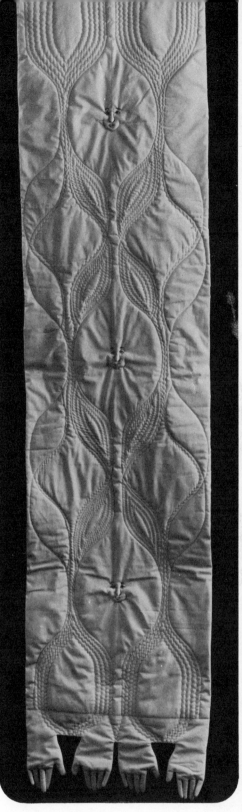

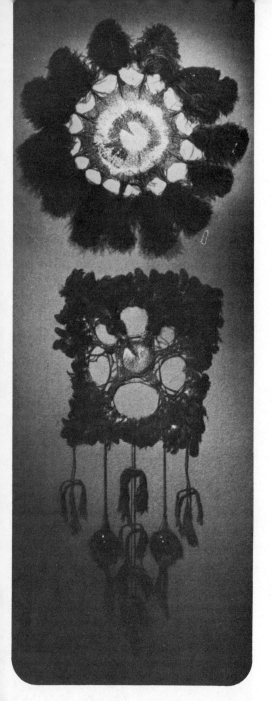

FEATHERED TOTEM
By Everett K. Sturgeon; photo by Grover Gilchrist

    Technique: Open-space embroidery. Centers done with floating couching, pearl cotton thread, and free-surface machine embroidery, or with embroidery floss in the bobbin and worked from the reverse side. Feathers and fringe added.

SWEET PENELOPE (*facing page*)
By Joan Blumenbaum

    Technique: Center image machine embroidered, except Penelope, the peas she is standing on, and the top of the pea pods. Center appliquéd to outer sections appliquéd together. Frame worked with satin stitch to form channels for trapunto work. Stuffed piece appliquéd to background shape.

    Fabric: Center, linen; frame, velvet.

SEWN PAINTINGS AND DRAWINGS

NUDES RECLINING
By Sas Colby

    Technique: Drawing done with straight stitch and free-surface machine embroidery. Satin stitch used for additional shapes. All shapes are appliquéd to background.

    Fabric: Silk, trimmed close to stitching to allow raw edge to fray. Page from *Silky Book,* a ten-page soft book of silk, collection of Fairtree Fine Crafts Institute.

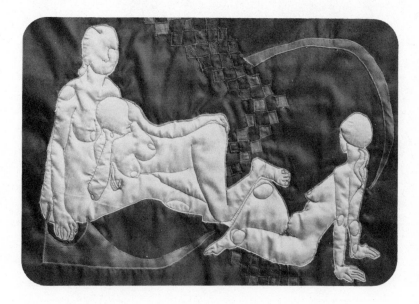

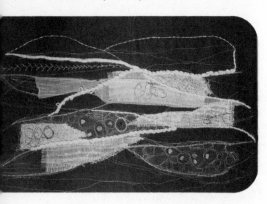

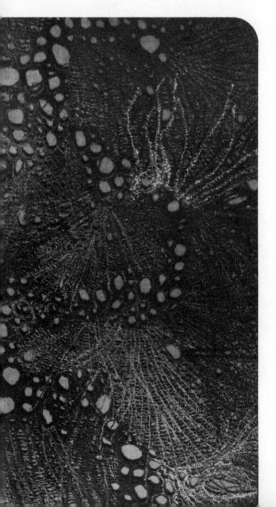

THE SEA
By Bucky King

Technique: Free-surface machine embroidery, straight stitch, and couching used as linear enrichment to appliqué. Fabrics chosen for textural qualities; contrasting background accents delicacy of stitched lines and appliquéd fabrics. Small stones and fine gold wire complete the work.

Fabric: White net and gauze on blue serge.

JOY WITH MACHINE EMBROIDERY
By Regina Bartley

Technique: Silk bouclé, homespun, heavy and fine yarns surface couched with zigzag stitch, nylon thread in spool and white in the bobbin. Webs formed with cut work and open-space embroidery and backed loosely with couched and pattern-stitched fabric. Stretched on frame.

SEA ANEMONE
By Everett K. Sturgeon; photo by Grover Gilchrist

Technique: Endless threads of yarn couched with zigzag stitch on soft puckering fabric, creating rich pebbled surface texture.

EXPLORATION *(facing page)*
By Patrick Ragland

Technique: Satin stitch, pattern stitch, varied stitch width satin stitch, zigzag stitch, straight stitch, free-surface machine embroidery, and open-space embroidery all used. Small strings, open square, and circles stitched first, and then assembled on covered metal bars attached to stitched and covered frame. Some swing free; others are stitched to each other. Fringe at the bottom achieved by cutting threads far from the fabric and tying them together.

Fabric: Felt.

Witch, PORTRAIT IN APPLIQUÉ *(facing page)*
By Margaret Cusack

Technique: Traced blow-up of subject placed on light table and outlined on fabric swatches; pieces then appliquéd into collage. Padding is polyester batting.

Fabric: Gabardine, cotton, linen, silk; any fabric or material.

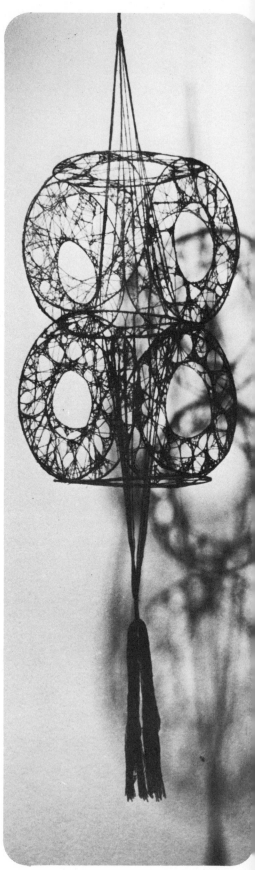

SCULPTURES

HANGING SCULPTURES: Fireworks II, Blue-Green Poem
By Everett K. Sturgeon

Technique: All pieces worked with free-surface machine embroidery over wire forms, stitched together to create whole form. Piano wire soldered together, thread machine stitched over it, and open-space machine stitching done from edge to edge of wires. By catching stitches in thread covering wires, lacy patterns are created.

Straight Arrow, SILK BIB
By Sas Colby

Technique: Free-surface machine embroidery on reclining figure used with appliqué, photo transfers, mirror embroidery, beads, sequins, labels, badges, and tassel.

Fabric: Various silks, crepes, and velvets.

Silver Medusa Head, SOFT SCULPTURE JEWELRY
By Margaret Cusack

Technique: Fabric stitched with free-surface machine embroidery and stuffed; hairs are stiffened with wire to retain forms. Roughly ten inches square.

Fabric: Silver satin; soft vinyl or leather.

Garden Dancers, SOFT SCULPTURE (DETAIL)
By Marjorie Moore

Technique: Design drawn with inks on fabric with quilted velvet and trapunto quilting.

Fabric: Unbleached muslin; velvet.

Snow Crystal Flower, SOFT SCULPTURE
By Priscilla Kepner Sage

> *Technique:*   Work developed with machine stitching and
> trapunto quilting, reinforced with wire armature
> to stand alone.
>
> *Fabric:*   Doubleknits.

Bunny Fur Form, HANGING SCULPTURE
By Priscilla Kepner Sage

> *Technique:*   Fabric worked with Italian quilting and trapunto,
> with hanging ropes and feathers.
>
> *Fabric:*   Satin, fur, rope, feathers.

Cloud Women, SOFT SCULPTURE
By Marjorie Moore

> *Technique:*   Figures are drawn, worked with trapunto quilting,
> and stuffed.
>
> *Fabric:*   Unbleached muslin.

suppliers

Embroidery Threads, Yarns, and Accessories

UNITED STATES

Department stores; yarn shops;
dime stores.

American Thread Corporation
350 Veterans Boulevard
Rutherford, NJ

American Crewel Studio *(mail order)*
Box 553
Westfield, NJ

Appleton Bros. of London
West Main Road
Little Crompton, RI 02837

Boutique Margot
26 W. 54th Street
New York, NY

Bucky King Embroideries, Unlimited
121 South Drive
Pittsburgh, PA 15238

The Dutch Nook
1609 College Place
Norfolk, VA 23517

The Needle's Point
1626 Macon Street
McLean, VA 22101

Selma's Art Needlework
1645 Second Avenue
New York, NY

Yarn Bazaar Yarncrafts Ltd.
3146 M Street N.W.
Washington, DC

Robin Hood Wool Shop
127 College Heights
Clemson, SC

Swiss Metrosene
34 S. Vine Street
Hinsdale, IL 60521

Handcraft from Europe
Box 372
Sausalito, CA

GREAT BRITAIN

Appleton Bros.
Church Street
Chiswick, London, W. 4

C & F Handcraft Suppliers
246 Stag Lane
Kingsbury, London, N.W. 9

Harrods Ltd. *(also fabrics)*
Knightsbridge, London, S.W. 1

John Lewis *(also fabrics)*
Oxford Street
London, W. 1

Louis Grosse Ltd.
36 Manchester Street
London, W. 1

Maccullocks & Wallis, Ltd.
25-26 Dering Street
London, W. 1

The Needlewoman
146 Regent Street
London, W. 1

The Royal School of Needlework
25 Princess Gate
London, S.W. 7

Christine Riley *(also fabrics)*
58 Barclay Street
Stonehaven, Kincardineshire

Dryad, Northgates
Leicester, L.E.I. 4 QR

Mace & Nairn *(also gold and
silver kid, whole skins only)*
89 Crane Street
Salisbury, Wilts.

The Hobby Horse
52 Montgomery Street
Eaglesham, Renfrewshire

Craftsman's Mark Ltd.
Dungannon Company
Tyrone, N. Ireland

J. Hyslop Bathgate & Company
Victoria Works
Galashiels, Scotland

T. M. Hunter
Sutherland Mills
Brora, Scotland

Fabrics

UNITED STATES

Local fabric and drapery shops;
department stores.

GREAT BRITAIN

John Lewis
Oxford Street
London, W. 1

Liberty & Company *(handwoven silk)*
Regent Street
London, W. 1

Mary Allen *(specialist supplier)*
Turditch, Derbyshire

Dicksons & Company, Ltd.
Dungannon Company
Tyrone, N. Ireland

Specialty Yarns

UNITED STATES

Craft Yarns of Rhode Island *(mail order)*
603 Mineral Spring Avenue
Pawtucket, RI 10862

Quicket
231 E. 53rd Street
New York, NY

Tahki Imports *(Greek, handspun)*
336 West End Avenue
New York, NY

Threadbare Unlimited
20 Cornelia
New York, NY

Lily Mills
Dept. H. W. H.
Shelby, NC 28150

Mexiskeins, Inc. *(Mexican, handspun)*
P. O. Box 1924
Missoula, MT 59801

Plastics

UNITED STATES

Almac Plastics
47-42 37th Street
Long Island City, NY 11101

Plasticrafts
2800 N. Speer
Denver, CO 80211

Port Plastics
180 Constitution Drive
Menlo Park, CA 94025

Canvas, Cotton, and Plastic Mesh

Local industrial bag suppliers

Natural Linen

UNITED STATES

Bon Bazaar, Inc. *(felt, all colors)*
149 Waverly Place
New York, NY 10014

Central Shippee *(burlap)*
35 Hamburg Turnpike
Bloomingdale, NJ

Utrecht Linen
32 Third Avenue
New York, NY

Homespun House
9024 Linblad Avenue
Culver City, CA 90230

Leather

UNITED STATES

Aerolyn Fabrics, Inc. *(gold and silver kid)*
900 Passaic Avenue
Harrison, NJ

MacLeather Company
424 Broome Street
New York, NY

Tandy Leather Company, Inc.
508 Sixth Avenue
New York, NY

P. O. Box 791
Fort Worth, TX 76101

GREAT BRITAIN

John Lewis
Furnishings Dept.
Oxford Street
London, W. 1

The Light Leather Company
*(gold and silver kid,
whole skins only)*
16 Soho Square
London, W. 1

R & AK Kohnstamm Ltd.
Randack Tannery
Croydon Road
Beckenham, Kent

Messrs. Pittard, Sherbrook Road
(kid, whole skins only)
Yeovil, Somerset

Decorations

UNITED STATES

Glori Bead Shop
172 W. 4th Street
New York, NY 10014

Sidney Coe, Inc.
65 W. 37th Street
New York, NY

Ararity
1021 R Street
Sacramento, CA

Bethlehem Imports
5231 Cushman Place
San Diego, CA 92110

Gloria's Glass Garden
Box 1990
N. Beverly Hills, CA 90213

GREAT BRITAIN

Bourne & Hollingsworth Ltd.
Oxford Street
London, W. 1

Ells & Farrier
5 Princess Street
London, W. 1

Rubans de Paris
39a Maddox Street
London, W. 1

Embroidery Patterns

UNITED STATES

Simplicity Pattern Company
200 Madison Avenue
New York, NY 10016

Swiss Bernina
34 Vine Street
Hinsdale, IL 60521

Craft and Related Organizations

UNITED STATES

American Crafts Council
Crafts Horizons magazine
44 W. 53rd Street
New York, NY

Embroiders' Guild of America, Inc.
20 E. 53rd Street
New York, NY

Embroidery Council of America, Inc.
20 E. 53rd Street
New York, NY

Museum Books, Inc.
48 E. 43rd Street
New York, NY

Museum of Contemporary Crafts
29 W. 53rd Street
New York, NY

School Arts
Crafts for Schools magazine
114 W. Riding Road
Cherry Hill, NJ

GREAT BRITAIN

The Crafts Centre of Great Britain
43 Earlham Street
London, W. C. 2

The Embroiderers' Guild
73 Wimpole Street
London, W. 1